Chester A. Arthur

Chester Alan Arthur (undated photograph)
Courtesy of the Library of Congress

CHESTER A. ARTHUR

The Accidental President

John M. Pafford

REGNERY
HISTORY

Regnery History™ is a trademark of Salem Communications Holding Corporation
Regnery® is a registered trademark of Salem Communications Holding Corporation

Cataloging-in-Publication data on file with the Library of Congress

ISBN 978-1-62157-595-5
ebook ISBN 978-1-62157-622-8

Published in the United States by
Regnery History
An imprint of Regnery Publishing
A Division of Salem Media Group
300 New Jersey Ave NW
Washington, DC 20001
www.RegneryHistory.com

Manufactured in the United States of America

10 9 8 7 6 5 4 3 2 1

Books are available in quantity for promotional or premium use. For information on discounts and terms, please visit our website: www.Regnery.com.

*To all who unexpectedly rise to new heights
above what most of their contemporaries believed possible*

CONTENTS

Preface   ix

CHAPTER 1
The Unexpected   1

CHAPTER 2
Early Years   5

CHAPTER 3
Political Rise   11

CHAPTER 4
Machine Politician   23

CHAPTER 5
Clash with Hayes   33

CHAPTER 6
Up to Second Place   37

CHAPTER 7
The New President   51

CHAPTER 8
Arthur and Race   65

CHAPTER 9
Taking Charge   79

CHAPTER 10
Conflicts Intensify   87

CHAPTER 11
Reforming the Armed Forces 101

CHAPTER 12
Central American Canal   115

CHAPTER 13
Foreign Policy   121

CHAPTER 14
Society   133

CHAPTER 15
1884 Election   157

CHAPTER 16
The Last Act   173

CHAPTER 17
Evaluation   181

Notes   187
Index   207

Preface

O nce the founding generation of American presidents—Washington, Adams, Jefferson, Madison, and Monroe—had retired from active leadership, presidents did not usually dominate public life until the twentieth century. From 1824 through the end of the nineteenth century, there were the towering figures of Andrew Jackson and Abraham Lincoln, whose marks on our country remain. But the presidents between Jackson and Lincoln and between Lincoln and Theodore Roosevelt left little historical impression. The average citizen may recognize their names but knows little else about them.

Their obscurity is perhaps understandable because they governed in relatively undramatic times—especially those three decades after the Civil War and before the emergence of the United States as a world power, though this was the time when the American economy boomed and the U.S. Armed Forces began ascending to the top tier.

Some of these forgotten presidents—William Henry Harrison, Zachary Taylor, James Garfield—were in office for too short a time to make their mark there. Franklin Pierce and James Buchanan failed to act decisively, leaving behind crises greater than they inherited. Andrew

Johnson, an inept leader, had little support and was almost removed from office. Ulysses S. Grant, a great military figure, was an incompetent president. Rutherford B. Hayes was honest and competent, but his administration was hampered by his controverted election and his pledge to serve only one term. Benjamin Harrison was a decent mediocrity. Best of all the presidents between Lincoln and Theodore Roosevelt was the rather bland Grover Cleveland, a conservative who has not been as appreciated as he deserves. He should be remembered as honest and effective.

And then there is Chester Alan Arthur, the most unlikely of our chief executives. The other "forgotten" presidents at least had achieved national prominence in the government or the armed forces, but Arthur had held no elective office prior to his election as vice president in 1880. His most important position, collector of the New York customs house, was powerful and lucrative but was hardly equivalent to that of a United States senator or a state governor. From his youth he had impressed people with his intelligence, charm, and organizational and administrative abilities, but his career had been sidetracked. In 1880 he was regarded as, at best, a competent, upper-tier lieutenant in the New York political machine of Roscoe Conkling. Yet as president, Arthur rose to an unexpected level of principle and accomplishment. Making his record more impressive is that about one year after assuming the presidency, he was diagnosed with Bright's disease, a debilitating kidney ailment for which there was no cure at that time.

Arthur's career is a cautionary tale of wandering after a promising start into professional paths that were lucrative, but not commensurate with the promise of his youth. Then he suddenly was given another chance when he became president after the assassination of Garfield.

CHAPTER 1

The Unexpected

Saturday, July 2, 1881, dawned more pleasant than the steamy, typical Washington, D.C., summer day it would become. James Garfield, who had been president for just under four months, planned to leave on the train at nine thirty in the morning from the Baltimore and Potomac station at Sixth and B Streets, N.W. (today the site of the National Gallery of Art), a short distance from the Executive Mansion, commonly called the White House. (Theodore Roosevelt would make that name official in 1901.)

Garfield looked forward to vacationing with his family and avoiding the unhealthy heat and humidity of midsummer Washington. They would travel north to New York City, sail up the Hudson River on the yacht of Cyrus Field, an entrepreneur known for promoting the transatlantic telegraph line, and spend the night at Field's Irvington mansion. The party then would cross into western Massachusetts for graduation ceremonies at Williams College, the president's alma mater, where he hoped eventually to send his two older sons. Next they would continue to Augusta, Maine, for the weekend with Secretary of State James G. Blaine. After a brief return to Washington, Garfield and his family then would spend August at their comfortable home on 160 acres in Mentor, Ohio, not far from Cleveland. The president looked forward to getting his administration into higher gear after the summer vacation. But it was not meant to be.

At about nine o'clock in the morning, Garfield left by carriage for the train station with Blaine but without security personnel. The Secret Service had been established a few years earlier after Abraham Lincoln's assassination, but presidential security came after fighting counterfeiting in the agency's priorities. The passage of fifteen years since Lincoln's death—considered a wartime aberration—had brought complacency. But political assassinations were a worldwide danger. During the 1870s, presidents José Balta of Peru, Gabriel García Moreno of Ecuador, and Juan Bautista Gill of Paraguay were slain, as was Sultan Abdul Aziz of Turkey. A few days after Garfield took office in March 1881, Tsar Alexander II of Russia fell victim to an assassin. Attempts had been made in recent years on the lives of Queen Victoria of the United Kingdom, King Alfonso XII of Spain, Emperor Napoleon III of France, and King Victor Emmanuel II of Italy. Yet on this day in July 1881, Garfield entered the train station accompanied only by the secretary of state and his sons—Harry, who was seventeen years old, and James, who was two years younger.

Inside the station waited Charles Julius Guiteau, a deluded, frustrated office-seeker, a ne'er-do-well who dreamed of distinction but always fell short and blamed his failures on others. In recent weeks he had stalked Garfield, getting close to him during a service at the Vermont Avenue Christian Church and while the president and Blaine walked the short distance from the White House to the secretary of state's house. Each time, Guiteau held back from striking. Now he was determined not to miss this opportunity to change history. He drew his weapon, a .44 caliber British Bulldog revolver, and as the two men passed him he fired two bullets at short range from behind. The first struck Garfield in the right arm. As he turned, Guiteau fired the second and fatal shot, hitting him in the back. As he tried to flee, Guiteau was grabbed by Robert Parker, a ticket agent, and Washington police officer Patrick Kearney.

Garfield's wound need not have been fatal. The bullet penetrated his back to the right of his spine, broke two ribs, and came to rest ten inches into his body without hitting any vital organs or severing any major blood vessels. But because he was president, Garfield attracted medical attention—not always healthy in those days. Doctors determined to find the bullet probed with unsterilized hands—introducing the infection which would kill him—without ever locating the bullet. This was infuriatingly bad practice by prominent physicians such as Smith Townsend, a District of Columbia health officer, and Doctor Willard Bliss ("Doctor" was his first name), a celebrated surgeon who had tended the dying President Lincoln. Many physicians, including these, still rejected Joseph Lister's antiseptic practices. Had Garfield's wounds been cleaned and left alone, he most likely would have survived the attack. But the attending doctors, stubbornly resistant to Lister's discoveries, caused the fatal infection to develop and spread.

The famed inventor Alexander Graham Bell was brought in to find the bullet using his new induction balance machine, which could detect metal within a human body. The machine failed to locate the bullet, probably because of the metal springs in Garfield's bed and because Dr. Bliss mistook where the bullet had lodged.[1]

Garfield's suffering was exacerbated by the humid heat of Washington. The navy did provide an early type of air conditioner for his room in the White House, but the temperature still was in the eighties and the air was heavy. After enduring these conditions for several weeks, Garfield insisted on being moved to Elberon on the northern New Jersey shore near Long Branch, a location he had enjoyed previously. He left Washington by special train on September 6, staying at the twenty-two-room summer home of his friend Charles G. Franklyn, a New York financier. At first, Garfield improved, buoyed by the fresh salt air and the views of the ocean, but given the wrongheaded medical treatment inflicted on him, the end was inevitable. He died at 10:35 p.m. on September 19, 1881.

The autopsy showed how wrong the doctors had been about the bullet's location. Dr. D. S. Lamb of the Army Medical Museum led the procedure, assisted by six of Garfield's medical men, including Dr. Bliss. The bullet was found, but not where the attending doctors thought it would be. It had entered the back and gone left, causing only limited damage. It was the unsterilized probing that had killed him.[2]

During the weeks after the shooting, Arthur spent most of the time at his home in New York City, staying away from Washington to avoid giving the impression that he was power-hungry or keeping a death watch. Arthur was hit hard by Garfield's death, but he rose to be president in fact, not just in name. Summoned to Arthur's home at a quarter past two in the morning on September 20, Judge John Brady of the New York Supreme Court administered the oath of office. Arthur then proceeded to Elberon and accompanied Garfield's body to Washington. There Chief Justice Morrison Waite of the U.S. Supreme Court administered the oath of office to the new president in an official ceremony.

Chester Alan Arthur now was president of the United States, arguably the most unlikely of the men who have held this office. Although he faced no major international or domestic crisis such as war or depression, he proved to be a president of intelligence and ability, one who deserves to rise in the esteem of the American people. The account of his transformation is fascinating and surprising.

CHAPTER 2

Early Years

Arthur was born on October 5, 1829, in North Fairfield, Vermont, near the border of Quebec, the fifth child and first son of Reverend William Arthur and Malvina Arthur, née Stone. William Arthur, born in County Antrim in northern Ireland in 1796, had immigrated as a young man to Canada, settling for a while in Quebec before moving south into Vermont. He was studying law when a dramatic conversion to Christ as Savior and Lord led to a new career as a Baptist pastor. Malvina was born in 1802 on a farm just south of the Canadian border.

Firm in his Christian profession, William Arthur tended to be imperious, sharp-tongued, and irritable, traits that resulted in a number of moves for the family—seven during Chester's early years—which ended in upstate New York. Chester responded well to his father's pushing him educationally, but in a more limited way to his spiritual expectations. Little is known about his religious beliefs, but it seems that the future president remained in the Christian fold while adopting a less rigorous, more private faith than that in which he was raised.

In September 1845, just short of his sixteenth birthday, Arthur entered Union College in Schenectady, New York, one of the first colleges to offer students curricular options. Instead of the standard classics, students could focus on natural science or engineering. Arthur, however, chose classics, studying Homer, Xenophon, Herodotus, Thucydides, Livy, Cicero, and Tacitus, along with algebra, plane and solid geometry, trigonometry, chemistry, political economy, moral philosophy, astronomy, botany, geology, and physiology.[1] The ordinary rigorous day began with breakfast and prayers at six thirty in the morning, continuing until the final study period at seven o'clock in the evening.[2] Foreshadowing his later career in law and then in politics, Arthur was president of the debating society.

He completed his degree requirements in three years, graduating in July 1848 as a member of Phi Beta Kappa, a distinction shared by only three other presidents: John Quincy Adams (Harvard 1787), Theodore Roosevelt (Harvard 1880), and George H. W. Bush (Yale 1948). Herbert Hoover had the requisite grades at Stanford, but engineering students were not honored with membership.[3] Arthur certainly did well at Union, although among the high caliber student body, he did not stand out.

To defray college expenses, he had taught school during the lengthy winter vacations. Now, degree in hand, Arthur returned to teaching to earn a living while studying privately for the bar examination. He spent a few months at the State and National Law School in Ballston Spa, New York. It is not clear why he did not complete the program there, but the most likely explanation was his need to generate income. He moved on to teach school in North Pownal in the southwestern corner of Vermont, and then served as principal of the academy in Cohoes, New York, near Albany.

During these years, he was studying privately for the bar, as was the option at that time for those unable or unwilling to attend a law school. To complete his preparation, Arthur moved to New York City, studying and working at the law office of E. D. Culver. In May 1854, he passed the bar examination and joined what then became the firm of Culver, Parker, and Arthur. He was a sharp young man on the rise in a growing part of the country during a dramatic time in American history. His handsome appearance, charming personality, and impressive stature (six feet, two inches) opened doors for him, and his intelligence and ability solidified his position, furthering his rise professionally and politically.

By the mid-1850s, the political party system had been torn apart by the failure of the Whigs to resolve their deep divisions over slavery. Northern Whigs favored ending the practice, while Southern Whigs supported its continuation. The party tore itself apart. Northern Whigs became the core of the new antislavery Republican Party, while Southern Whigs joined the Democrats, who called for each state to set its own policy on slavery.

Arthur had been a Whig, but he saw that the party's failure to take a clear stand on slavery doomed it to irrelevance. His own opposition to slavery, which he shared with his father, led him into the Republican Party in 1854, shortly after its organization. He would soon have an opportunity to put his principles into practice.

In 1854, Lizzie Jennings, a black school teacher, was ousted from a New York City streetcar that was reserved for "whites only." She protested through the legal system. Arthur took the case, arguing that nothing his client had done warranted her being expelled from the streetcar. The jury agreed and awarded Jennings $250, and the case prompted the decision later that year to desegregate public transportation in New York City. The tide of freedom was rising slowly, but perceptibly.

On the national stage, 1854 was the year of the Kansas-Nebraska Act, a disastrously flawed attempt to placate the South and avoid conflict by opening more territory to the possible expansion of slavery. The Missouri Compromise of 1820 had excluded slavery from the Louisiana territory north of the 36° 30′ parallel except for Missouri, where slavery would be legal. Southern opinion considered it too restrictive and pushed for this new arrangement. The new law allowed the Kansas and Nebraska territories, although north of the Missouri Compromise line, to vote for or against slavery. It was bitterly opposed by those who considered slavery wrong but was supported by key Democratic Party leaders such as President Franklin Pierce and the increasingly prominent senator Stephen Douglas of Illinois. With the Democrats calling for compromise and the

Ellen Lewis Herndon Arthur, 1837–1880
Courtesy of the Library of Congress

Whigs unable to unite on a stance, the way was clear for a new party. Northern Whigs were the core of the Republican Party—born in 1854, a major political force by 1856, and the dominant party by 1860. An enthusiastic Republican, Arthur was a young man clearly on the rise.

His personal life too was brightening. In 1856, Arthur fell in love with Ellen Lewis Herndon of Fredericksburg, Virginia. Known as Nell, she was the daughter of the famed explorer and ship captain William L. Herndon. While visiting New York, she was introduced to Arthur by Dabney Herndon, her cousin and his friend. The spark was evident, but she was only seventeen at the time. In the interim, Arthur headed west to Kansas with his friend and fellow attorney, Henry G. Gardiner, attracted by the opportunity of land speculation. Arthur had purchased land near Leavenworth.

A letter he wrote to Nell on August 30, 1857, from St. Joseph, Missouri, reveals a side of Arthur seen by few. This is the only surviving missive from him to her written during their three years of courtship. He mentions his business in Kansas, but most of the letter expresses his love and longing for Nell. Also evident is his spiritual faith and a rather poetic side:

> This is your birth-day—my own precious darling—my own Nell. The remembrance came with my first awaking in the early morning—as the thought of you always does and as I kissed your dear image, darling, my heart was full to over-flowing with love and prayer for you! And when I looked out, and saw it was a glad, bright morning and everything looked fresh & beautiful, I thought it a happy omen! How full of joy & happiness the world seemed to me, for I felt that you are my own Nell—that you love me! I said "I am content." I was happy and thanked God that he had so blessed me!
>
> The day has fulfilled its morning promise, it has been most bright and beautiful even to the last rays of its gorgeous sunset, still lingering in the sky.
>
> Who is there, dear, darling, Nell, who can, today, so anx-iously & lovingly wish you all earthly happiness—richer blessings with each returning year & God's blessing and protecting care, here & hereafter—as your own loving Ches-ter—May these blessings all be yours and, oh, if any part of that earthly happiness be in my keeping, my darling, my pre-cious one, it is a precious, sacred trust dearer than life itself!

Arthur continues in the same manner, ending with an outpouring of his love for her:

> I know you are thinking of me now. I feel the pulses of your love answering to mine. If I were with you now, you would go & sing for me: "Robin Adair"—then you would come & sit by me—you would put your arms around my neck and press your soft sweet lips over my eyes—I can feel them now.

Yes darling, my heart is indeed full to night, full of love for you, of happiness and gratitude for your love. Swelling with all these recollections & with the thought, that with God's blessing, I shall soon hold you to my heart again! The hours grow longer every day.

Good night. May God bless & keep you always my darling.

Your own Chester.[4]

This feeling was real and lasting. There would be strains on their relationship as Arthur became absorbed in his career, but Nell was his true love; that never changed.

While they were probing their prospects, word arrived that Nell's father had perished in the worst commercial ship disaster in American history. William Herndon was captain of the steamer *Central America*, which had sailed for New York from the Caribbean side of Panama with 575 passengers and crew and thirty thousand pounds of gold from California. In mid-September 1857 off Cape Hatteras, North Carolina, the ship was caught in an autumn hurricane. Herndon exhibited cool heroism in supervising the transfer of 152 women and children to another vessel. Having done all he could, he stayed with those who could not be saved and went down with his ship. In tribute to his valor, towns in Virginia and Pennsylvania were named after him, as were three naval ships—a destroyer in 1925, then another destroyer and a transport during World War II.[5]

Arthur concluded that "Bleeding Kansas," torn by violent strife between pro-slavery and anti-slavery forces, was no place to settle and raise a family, and with Nell's loss of her father, he returned to New York and managed the legal and business affairs of the Herndon family. When he married Nell at Calvary Episcopal Church on October 25, 1859, his personal life and his professional life were on the upswing. Soon the Civil War would put a strain on the first and greatly enhance the second.

CHAPTER 3

Political Rise

As the 1850s neared their end, prospects for avoiding civil strife were fading. For several decades, the South had been falling behind the North in wealth and in population. Industrial development brought the Northern states more wealth, more jobs, more people, and more political power. The North supported high tariffs to protect business and jobs from foreign competition. Southerners, dependent on agricultural exports—especially cotton, tobacco, and indigo—called for low tariffs, which permitted them to purchase foreign manufactured items for less than the cost of Northern goods and encouraged these overseas sellers to import what was grown in the South. This difference had been producing strains for years, and civil strife had come close in the 1830s during Andrew Jackson's presidency. As long as Southerners had equal representation in the Senate, they grumbled but stayed in the union. By the end of the 1850s, though, the political situation was becoming unstable and war loomed.

In 1858 and 1859, Minnesota and Oregon entered the union as free states, ending the balance of free and slave states and putting the South on edge. Secession was more and more likely. A good number of

Southerners opposed slavery, but for most of them solidarity with their state would prevail over national unity once secession began.

Arthur's career took a major upturn with the election of Edwin D. Morgan as governor of New York in 1858. A successful banker and businessman before entering politics, Morgan was the lieutenant of Thurlow Weed, the most powerful figure in New York politics for years. Morgan would be reelected governor in 1860 and later serve a term in the United States Senate. The Weed-Morgan organization would eventually lose a power struggle for control of the New York Republican Party to Roscoe Conkling, denying Morgan a second term in the Senate. But in the late 1850s and into the 1860s, Morgan was at the peak of his power. He appointed Arthur to serve as New York's engineer in chief with the rank of brigadier general in the state militia. As the likelihood of war between the North and the South grew, Arthur was determined to join what he saw as the right side.

The election of 1860 was of unusual significance. Four major contenders vied for votes as the country faced secession and war. Desperately attempting to hold their party together, the Democrats convened in Charleston, South Carolina, hoping that Southerners would see this as a gesture of goodwill and that division of both the party and of the country could be avoided. The Southerners, though, wanted more than a gesture. They demanded a plank in the party platform protecting slavery in the territories. Failing to get it, they walked out. Party leaders wanted to avoid conflict, but they could not go that far. Senator Stephen Douglas of Illinois was the leading candidate for president, but on ballot after ballot he failed to secure the requisite number of votes. Finally, after trying fifty-seven times to choose a candidate, the convention adjourned, determined to try again.

Meanwhile, the Republicans gathered in Chicago from May 16 to 18 for their second nominating convention. The leading contender for their presidential nomination was Senator William Seward, a former governor of New York, but he faced a strong challenge from Abraham Lincoln of Illinois, a successful lawyer who had served three terms in the state legislature and a term in the U.S. House of Representatives. Lincoln had shot to national prominence in his 1858 U.S. Senate race against Stephen A. Douglas. On the first ballot in Chicago, Seward led with 173½ votes, short of the requisite 233; Lincoln was second with 102, and all other contenders were well below them. The shift to Lincoln was evident on the second ballot, and he won on the third. Senator Hannibal Hamlin of Maine was selected as his running mate. The party opposed slavery in the territories but did not call for its elimination in the slave states.

Those who hoped to keep the country together by avoiding any stand on slavery met at Baltimore on May 9 and 10 as the Constitutional Union Party. Their determination to straddle the slavery issue was evident in their party's platform: "Resolved: that it is both the part of patriotism and of duty to recognize no political principle other than the Constitution of the country, the Union of the States and the enforcement of the laws."[1] Actually, this brief statement constituted the platform of the party.

This avoidance of a principled stance also was reflected in their ticket. The presidential nominee was John Bell of Tennessee, a slave owner who had been Speaker of the U.S. House of Representatives, secretary of war, and a member of the U.S. Senate. His running mate was the antislavery Edward Everett of Massachusetts—a scholar, former governor, former secretary of state, and former U.S. senator.

The Democrats, now missing most of their Southern delegates, convened in Baltimore from June 18 to 23 and nominated Douglas on their second ballot. Hoping to avoid the disruption of their party and country, they nominated Herschel Johnson, a former U.S. senator and governor of Georgia, for vice president. Their platform protected slavery, although it did call for each territory to determine for itself whether to be free or slave.

On June 23, also in Baltimore, the Southern Democrats organized themselves as the National Democrats, rather a misnomer since their appeal beyond the slave states was minimal. Here they nominated John Breckinridge, the sitting vice president under James Buchanan. Hoping to spread their appeal beyond the South, they nominated for vice president Senator Joseph Lane of Oregon. The new party clearly supported the continuation of slavery where it was legal, but called for the territories to determine for themselves whether to be free or to permit slavery.

It was clear to the voters that the Republicans opposed slavery while the National (Southern) Democrats supported it. The (Northern) Democrats opposed slavery but were content to let each state determine its own law on the matter. The Constitutional Union Party avoided the issue altogether. Most voters well understood how high the stakes were.

There was both concern and hope that no party could win a majority of the electoral vote and that the House of Representatives would select the president, as it had done in 1824. This did not occur. The popular vote was splintered, Lincoln leading with 1,865,593 votes, 39.8 percent of the total. Behind him were Douglas (1,382,713, 29.5 percent), Breckinridge (848,356, 18.1 percent), and Bell (592,906, 12.6 percent). But Lincoln's electoral vote was solid, as he carried eighteen states with 180 electoral votes. Breckinridge won eleven states with seventy-two electoral votes, followed by Bell, who won thirty-nine electoral votes from three states. Although Douglas finished second in the popular vote, the wide dispersal of his supporters left him with only Missouri's twelve electoral votes.[2]

Former presidents John Tyler and Franklin Pierce, as well as President Buchanan, backed Breckinridge, but for different reasons. Tyler owned slaves and would become a member of the Confederate Congress. Pierce and Buchanan opposed slavery personally, but believed that it was constitutionally protected and that civil strife could be avoided through placating the South. After secession, they supported the Union.

The election of Lincoln was the last straw for the determined Southern nationalists. Now loyalty to their states would trump allegiance to the United States. The exodus was led by South Carolina, which seceded just weeks later in December. In January, Mississippi, Florida, Alabama, Georgia, and Louisiana followed. On February 4, a convention in Montgomery, Alabama, formally established the Confederate States of America, with Jefferson Davis of Mississippi as president and Alexander Stephens of Georgia as vice president. Still, there were those in both the

North and the South who hoped the Rubicon had not been crossed and that a peaceful resolution still was possible.

Those hopes vanished on April 12 when Confederate forces in South Carolina opened fire on Fort Sumter in Charleston Harbor. With no hope of reinforcement or evacuation and under continual bombardment, the fort surrendered the next day. War now was a reality. Virginia, North Carolina, Texas, Arkansas, and Tennessee soon followed their fellow Southerners into the new country.

Arthur, both patriotic and ambitious, wanted a combat assignment but faced two obstacles. Governor Morgan, appealing to his sense of duty, urged him to stay on as engineer in chief, a position in which he could contribute more to victory than he could in a combat position. And Nell's family lived in Virginia. The conflicting loyalties put a strain on their marriage, which Arthur's abstention from combat might mitigate.

Chester Arthur had joined the New York militia in February 1858 as a brigade judge advocate. Militia officers received their appointments primarily because of their political connections. Arthur was one of the minority of highly capable men who rose through this political patronage system. Although political influence never disappeared during the conflict, the realities of fighting a major war caused a reevaluation of the key qualities for military command. From what is known of him, his motive was probably a combination of genuine patriotism as the prospect of a war with the South became likely and the recognition that service in a wartime army was conducive to rapid political and professional advancement. Additionally, as a healthy young man, the prospect of adventure most likely also moved him. In January 1861, the election of Lincoln and the beginning of secession having made war almost certain, Arthur was promoted to brigadier general and appointed as acting assistant quartermaster general. In February 1862, he moved up to inspector general.

A few months later, Arthur inspected New York troops stationed at Fredericksburg and on the Chickahominy River in Virginia, south of Richmond. This was a quiet sector at the time he was there. His charge was to bring the New York regiments up to full strength with the hope of remaining with the army in the field through the upcoming battles, but he received an urgent recall to New York from Governor Morgan. He was disappointed, but obeyed.

The Peninsula Campaign continued with Union forces under General George McClellan as he mounted an unsuccessful campaign to seize the Confederate capital of Richmond. The attempt failed, thwarted by General Robert E. Lee's skill and McClellan's excessive caution. Three more years of war lay ahead.

In July, Arthur was promoted again, now to quartermaster general of the New York militia.

The future certainly appeared bright for Arthur in the final months of 1862. In his mid-thirties, he had done well in a responsible, demanding position, showing initiative and the capacity to handle demanding duties. Fear of a Confederate naval attack on New York City gave him the opportunity to demonstrate his organizational skills and, possibly, combat ability. Arthur ordered to full strength the New York militia forces manning the harbor forts and ensured that the guns, although old, were supplied with shells. The city's defenses were well prepared for an attack that never happened. We know now that such an attack was unlikely, but it was feared at the time as a possibility. Arthur received plaudits, but professional and personal troubles were in the offing.

New York's volatile political arena, which had welcomed Arthur, now turned unfriendly. Thurlow Weed was on the decline before the rising power of Roscoe Conkling. Further complicating prospects for the Weed-Morgan organization were Confederate victories on the battlefield, which strengthened the hand of the Democrats, who supported a negotiated settlement of the war. Lee led the Army of Northern Virginia to victory over a succession of Union generals, defeating McClellan in the Peninsula Campaign outside of Richmond in the spring of 1862. He routed John Pope at the Second Battle of Bull Run in August and invaded Maryland. Although checked at Antietam by McClellan in September, Lee ended the year with a solid win over Ambrose

Burnside at Fredericksburg, Virginia. After Antietam, Lincoln announced the Emancipation Proclamation, freeing the slaves in the rebellious states and giving the North a moral rationale for the war and a public relations boost at home and abroad. By no means, however, were Lincoln's troubles over.

These Confederate successes gave credence to the Democrats' charges that the Lincoln administration was incompetent in its conduct of the war. Though the Democrats supported the Union, they opposed conscription and the suspension of habeas corpus, the right of those charged with crimes to be informed of the charges against them or be set free. By executive order, Lincoln suspended habeas corpus for those suspected of being Confederate operatives.[3]

The Democrats' 1862 gubernatorial nominee in New York, Horatio Seymour, had served a term as governor back in the mid-1850s. Seymour opposed the Emancipation Proclamation and called for a negotiated settlement of the war. The Democrats' opposition to Lincoln carried Seymour back into the governorship. Nationally, the Republicans managed to keep control of the Senate and the House, losing three seats in the House. The Democrats gained thirty-eight House seats, mostly from the disappearance of third parties, raising their confidence that in 1864 they would defeat Lincoln and again control Washington. They called for a peaceful settlement of the war, letting the South go. The Republicans remained adamant that the Union must be restored, and slavery ended in all states. For a while in the summer of 1864, Lincoln's defeat seemed likely. By the time of the election, the tide of the war had turned, and Union victory was in sight. Lincoln was reelected, and the Republicans regained the governorship of New York.

But as 1862 drew to a close, the prospects for the Union and for Republicans were bleak. Because of the change in New York state government, Arthur had to resign his post as of the end of the year.

His service was lauded by Governor Morgan:

> During the first two years of the Rebellion he was my chief reliance in the duties of equipping and transporting

troops and munitions of war. In the position of Quarter Master General he displayed not only great executive ability and unbending integrity, but great knowledge of Army Regulations. He can say No (which is important) without giving offence.[4]

Arthur also was commended by General S. V. Talcott, his successor, who was appointed by Seymour:

> I found on entering on the discharge of my duties, a well organized system of labor and accountability, for which the State is chiefly indebted to my predecessor, General Chester A. Arthur, who by his practical good sense and unremitting exertion, at a period when everything was in confusion, reduced the operations of this department to a matured plan, by which large amounts of money were saved to the government, and great economy of time secured in carrying out the details of the same.[5]

Early in 1863, personal tragedy befell the Arthurs with the death of their two-and-a-half-year-old son, William, from a brain hemorrhage. Both parents suffered grievously. Arthur castigated himself that he might have contributed to the condition by being too demanding of the lad and determined to be different with future children. Brighter times did lie ahead. A vital part of bringing in these brighter times was the birth of Chester Alan Arthur II on July 25, 1864. Called Alan, he brought great joy to his parents. He would grow to a strapping six feet, four inches and graduate from Princeton in 1885, but, overindulged by his parents, he never developed his intelligence and talents as he could have. A daughter, Ellen Herndon Arthur, known as "Nell" like her mother, was born on November 21, 1871. She married, settled in New York City, lived a rather uneventful life, and died in 1915.

In 1863, Arthur returned to his successful law practice but looked to politics as the likeliest way to enhance his status and income. In 1864, the Republicans regained the governor's office in New York with the victory of Reuben Fenton, and Arthur applied for the position of inspector general. Holding this office would give him a sense of patriotism without harming his relationship with his wife as a combat assignment would, and it would restore him to a position of prestige and stature. Though the office was not lucrative, it would permit him to continue his law practice.[6] Fenton, however, was in the radical wing of the Republican Party, opposed to conservatives such as Weed, Morgan, and Arthur. Determined to control his administration, Fenton rejected Arthur's application. The conservatives still were powerful, as had been shown by Edwin Morgan's election to the United States Senate the year before. The fight for control of the New York Republican Party in 1866 would be bitter.

Though defeat seemed possible for Lincoln in the 1864 election, we can see that the defeat of the South was inevitable. Its inferiority in population and economic power and its failure to gain foreign recognition and possible intervention made victory a futile hope. Yet in the summer of 1864, that was not clear. What most Americans saw then was the inability of the Union army to defeat Lee and seize Richmond, as well as William T. Sherman's failure to subdue Georgia. The Democrats promised an end to bloodshed by recognizing Southern independence and accepting the continuance of slavery there. But in September everything changed dramatically. Sherman took Atlanta and launched his dramatic march to the sea. A victorious end of the war in sight, Lincoln was reelected.

The assassination of Abraham Lincoln in 1865 made Andrew Johnson president. A Democrat who supported the administration's determination to win the Civil War, he had been put on the ticket with Lincoln the previous year to bring in Democrats who rejected their party's call for a negotiated settlement. The nomination of Johnson had been an excellent move and had helped the ticket win, but now Johnson had a limited base of support. Republicans did not see him as one of them, and Democrats considered him a traitor. Johnson's weakness limited Republicans' influence in New York.

The Weed organization mounted a major effort in 1866 to block Governor Fenton's bid for renomination and to regain control of the party. It fell short, and Thurlow Weed was finished as the dominant Republican in the state. Close to seventy years old, he retired from active politics and for a short time edited a newspaper. He remained a keen observer of the political landscape until close to the time of his death in 1882.

During the years immediately after the end of the Civil War, Roscoe Conkling rose from mere importance in the New York Republican Party to dominance. He had been born in Albany in October 1829—the same month and year as Arthur—into a prominent family. His father was an attorney who had been elected to the U.S. House of Representatives and then appointed as a federal judge. The son, too, entered the legal profession and was among the first Republicans. He was elected mayor of Utica and in 1858 won a seat in the U.S. House of Representatives. He was reelected in 1860, lost in 1862, then came back with victories in 1864 and 1866. Later, in 1867, Conkling defeated Ira Harris, a Weed supporter, for a U.S. Senate seat—another sign that a new political machine had risen to control the state.

This new political reality was evident in the late 1860s. Thurlow Weed was out as a political power. Edwin Morgan would finish his U.S. Senate term, but he lost his reelection bid to Reuben Fenton in January 1869. Although Fenton won this contest, he clearly no longer was the power he had been. Roscoe Conkling—charming, charismatic, and ruthless—now dominated New York politics and was growing in stature on the national stage.[7]

Arthur's prospects brightened. From both conviction and recognition of the new political realities, he tied himself to Conkling. He would prosper financially, socially, and politically, but from the standpoint of service to principle, the coming decade and a half would be a bleak period in Arthur's life.

The career of the Democrat William Magear "Boss" Tweed was peaking. He controlled Tammany Hall, and therefore politics in New York City, from 1866 to 1871. The Society of Tammany dated back to

1789, when it was formed as a patriotic organization, taking its name from a Delaware Indian chief known for his wisdom. By the time of Boss Tweed, it was a prototypical big-city machine, thriving on diverse forms of corruption and using part of its illicit income to help many people in need by providing jobs, food, and fuel for poor people—especially poor immigrants—thereby gaining their votes. Bribery, physical intimidation, and election fraud further strengthened the power of the Tweed machine. Opposition came from the Republican organization and from reform Democrats. This opposition finally would succeed in breaking Tweed's power in 1871 with his arrest, trial, and conviction on 204 misdemeanor charges. He spent only one year in prison, but he would not recover power. Tammany would recover, though, under John Kelly and Richard Croker and reassert its power before being broken in the 1930s by Mayor Fiorello La Guardia.

During these years in the second half of the 1860s and in the 1870s, Republicans generally controlled the state government in New York while the Tammany Hall Democrats held New York City. Under these circumstances, the making of deals was by no means rare. Apparently exemplifying this, in 1869 Arthur was selected as counsel for the New York City Tax Commission. He resigned a few months later, in the summer of 1870. Arthur said nothing of this episode and no definitive record of his tenure is known. There is no doubt that the Tweed machine controlled the government in New York City, including the tax commission. Perhaps the amount of corruption he saw from the inside of city government was too much for the admittedly ethically shaky Arthur of these years. He returned to his private law practice, but not for long.

CHAPTER 4

Machine Politician

In 1871, Arthur was appointed by President Grant to the far more lucrative post of collector of the Port of New York. Although Grant made the appointment, it was Conkling who decided who got it. The Port of New York, collecting about seventy-five percent of American trade duties and employing more than a thousand people, was one of the most important patronage prizes in the country. Although officially under the authority of the secretary of the treasury, the custom house was dominated by the collector, whose fiefdom was only loosely supervised by the administration in Washington. Receiving a handsome salary and a percentage of the fees charged to shippers who did not pay the correct tariff for goods entering New York, Arthur took in more than fifty thousand dollars a year at a time when the president's salary was fifty thousand dollars and the compensation of the vice president, cabinet members, and Supreme Court justices stood at ten thousand. Members of Congress lagged farther behind at $7,500. Even in that era of far more limited government and lower taxes and spending, there was an ample public trough at which to feed. Arthur held a powerful and lucrative position, but he assuredly was part of the Conkling machine.

Arthur was an honest collector in the sense that he did not accept graft and he did not steal money, but the employees of the custom house understood that they were expected to contribute financially to the Republican Party and to be loyal to it and to the collector.[1] Estimates of how much was to be "contributed" vary, but the figure probably was between 2 percent and 5 percent of each person's salary. Civil service reform was gaining support at this time, although success for the cause was years in the future.

The fortunes of the Conkling machine might have been a less elevated cause than preserving the union and ending slavery, but the sterling qualities Arthur had evinced during the Civil War surfaced at the custom house. He was an efficient administrator, running the office without the glitches and bottlenecks that could have hampered the smooth functioning of the country's biggest port. He also brought a certain panache to the post. He was a tall, handsome man, well read, convivial, and charming. But as he had demonstrated during the Civil War, he also could be a powerful adversary. During his years as collector, Arthur increased his influence and prosperity, without, however, developing as the leader he could have been based on the intelligence, skill, and independent strength that would come to the fore after the assassination of Garfield thrust him onto a grander stage.

Not long after Arthur settled into his new post, the election of 1872 seized the country's attention. The still popular Civil War hero Ulysses Grant was finishing his first term as president and was determined to win a second. Although he personally was not corrupt, in government he was a bad judge of character, choosing too many men who were corrupt or incompetent or both. There were honest and capable men in the administration, but knowledge of its failure to set and maintain high standards was spreading. It was good for Grant's campaign that most of the scandals would not become public until after the election. Still, the odor of corruption was strong enough to rouse opposition to Grant within Republican ranks.

On May 1, an impressive collection of anti-Grant Republicans gathered in Cincinnati to form a new party. Among them were senators

Charles Sumner of Massachusetts and Carl Schurz of Missouri, the literary figures William Cullen Bryant and James Russell Lowell, and the journalist Whitelaw Reid. Calling themselves the Liberal Republican Party, they met to nominate a ticket for the November election and to write a platform. For five ballots, no candidate could win the top spot. Leading at first was Charles Francis Adams, ambassador to the United Kingdom during the Civil War, the son of John Quincy Adams, and the grandson of John Adams. Second was Horace Greeley, the owner and publisher of the *New York Herald*, followed by Senator Lyman Trumbull of Illinois, Justice David Davis of the U.S. Supreme Court, and Governor Benjamin Gratz Brown of Missouri. On the sixth ballot, Greeley won, and he selected Brown as his running mate.

The party platform denounced the corruption in the Grant administration, which was now attracting attention, and advocated for civil service as the alternative to partisan patronage. The ending of remaining Civil War bitterness would be furthered by giving full amnesty to all former Confederates and fully reintegrating the Southern states. The platform also called for a single presidential term and for monetary reform getting the country away from unbacked paper.[2]

While Greeley had a brilliant record in the newspaper business, he was a rather bizarre choice as a presidential candidate. Greeley flip-flopped on the Civil War, first calling for letting the South go peacefully, then demanding total victory by the North. He also had dabbled in such causes as spiritualism and vegetarianism.[3]

On June 5 and 6, the Republicans convened in Philadelphia, where on the first ballot Grant was nominated for a second term. The incumbent vice president, former Speaker of the House Schuyler Colfax, was dropped from the ticket because of his involvement in the Crédit Mobilier scandal. Ostensibly a construction company, Crédit Mobilier actually was a dummy corporation set up by Union Pacific executives. Union Pacific paid Crédit Mobilier exorbitant amounts of money that went into the pockets of those who controlled it and as bribes to key congressional leaders. For their roles in the scam, representatives Oakes Ames of

Massachusetts and James Brooks of New York were censured by the House, and Senator James Patterson of New Hampshire was expelled. Senator Conkling and Speaker of the House James G. Blaine were cleared of all charges. The evidence against Colfax, while not conclusive, was substantial enough to cost him his place on the ticket, which was filled by Senator Henry Wilson of Massachusetts.[4]

The Democrats met in Baltimore on July 9 and 10. In an unprecedented move by a major party, they endorsed the ticket of the breakaway Liberal Republicans. In the balloting for president, Greeley won 686 of the 725 votes on the first ballot. The nomination then was made unanimous.[5] The Democrats were convinced that the split in Republican ranks would doom Grant's reelection. This would prove to be one of the worst political miscalculations on record: seriously underestimating Grant's popularity and badly overestimating Greeley's political skills.

A small group of Democrats who opposed their party's endorsement of Greeley and Brown met in Louisville, Kentucky, on September 3, calling themselves the Straight-Out Democratic Party. They selected Charles O'Connor of New York as their standard-bearer, with Charles Francis Adams as his running mate. O'Connor refused the nomination, but that was rejected and his name remained on the ballot.[6]

The drive to enfranchise women was picking up steam in 1872, although a few more decades would pass before it prevailed nationwide. The suffragette leader Susan B. Anthony spoke at the three major conventions that year. Only the Republicans gave a nod to her cause, referring in their platform to "obligations to the loyal women of America."

A more dramatic thrust was made that year by Victoria Woodhull, who became the first woman candidate for president. Her politics were very much left of center. Earlier in 1872, she and her sister, Tennessee C. Claflin, had founded a chapter of the International Workingmen's Association, a Marxist organization calling for violent revolution and the abolition of capitalism. They also advocated free love and spiritualism, causes that led to the revocation of their charter. Woodhull later that year was instrumental in organizing the Equal Rights Party, which held its national convention on May 10 in New York City. She electrified the 668 delegates as she announced that a new revolutionary era was dawning in this country—the old system would be overthrown and replaced.[7] The convention enthusiastically nominated her for president, with the great civil rights leader and former slave Frederick Douglass as her running mate. This rather questionable honor he rejected. Douglass did support suffrage for women, but as part of a broader movement which included full civil rights for blacks. Concerned that the Equal Rights Party was too narrowly focused, he endorsed Grant.[8]

Among the twenty-three planks in the party platform were those calling for nationalizing railroads, for removing land, mineral, and water resources from private ownership, guaranteed employment for all, and the establishment of a single worldwide government.[9]

The charismatic Woodhull was not yet thirty-five years old—the minimum age for serving as president—though her youth was not her only problem. At that time, only the territories of Wyoming and Utah had opened voting to women. Adding to her woes, she failed to gather the required petition signatures and to pay the filing fees and legal expenses for appearing on ballots.[10] The time for successful women political candidates still lay in the future. In 1872, women leaders divided their votes. For example, Susan B. Anthony, a former school teacher, leader in the temperance movement, and now in the forefront of the demand for women's suffrage, supported Grant. Belva Lockwood, who in 1879 would become the first woman to appear as an attorney before the Supreme Court, endorsed Greeley.[11]

The major-party candidates caused much dismay for a wide swath of the voting public. Alexander Stephens of Georgia, the former Confederate vice president and now a member of the U.S. House of Representatives, said that Grant versus Greeley was a choice between hemlock and strychnine.[12] Grant was vulnerable, but Greeley was too inept a campaigner to take advantage of his opponent's weakness. On November 5, Grant won 3,597,132 popular votes and 286 electoral votes to Greeley's 2,834,079 popular votes and 63 electoral votes. The Straight-Out

Democratic Ticket gained 29,489 votes. Greeley died on November 29, before the Electoral College convened. His electoral votes were eventually parceled out among four Democratic Party alternatives.

Into the mid-1870s, Arthur continued his service as collector of the Port of New York as an able, efficient, and loyal officer in the Conkling machine. This period of his life was marked by financial and social success, but was limited by his settling in as an upper-level machine politician.

In 1874, the Democrat Samuel Tilden won the New York gubernatorial election. A successful attorney, he had served in the state assembly and was elected in 1866 as chairman of the New York State Democratic Party. Honest and courageous, if rather bland, he led a crusade against the New York City political machine run by fellow Democrat Boss Tweed. This reputation for fighting corruption was key to his election as governor in 1874. Now the chief executive of the state with the largest population, Tilden shot to the front of the pack of contenders for the Democratic presidential nomination in 1876. There was optimism among the party faithful that the stench of scandal rising from the Grant administration could return the presidency to the Democrats for the first time since Buchanan gave way to Lincoln back in March 1861.

The Democrats' hopes for change were met by the Republican conviction that the country still preferred them, that the Lincoln legacy was stronger than weaknesses evident in the Johnson and Grant administrations. Leading in the battle for the Republican nomination was Speaker of the House James G. Blaine of Maine. Contesting his ambition were several powerful and equally ambitious leaders, the most prominent of whom were senator and former governor Oliver Morton of Indiana; Secretary of the Treasury Benjamin Bristow, who had served under Grant in the Civil War; and Arthur's patron, Senator Roscoe Conkling. Poised in the wings should the convention deadlock was Governor Rutherford B. Hayes of Ohio, who had distinguished himself as a Civil War general. Grant was ostensibly adhering to the unwritten two-term limit on presidents, a tradition begun by Washington. There is some dispute as to whether he genuinely had stepped aside or whether he was hoping for a chance to respond to a call for a third term. There are indications that he would have welcomed the convention's call, but that call never came—not in 1876 or in 1880.

When the Republicans convened from June 14 to 16 in Cincinnati, 379 votes were needed for the nomination. On the first ballot, Blaine won 285, Morton 124, Bristow 113, Conkling 99, and Hayes 61. On the next five ballots, Blaine increased his total, reaching 308 on the sixth—still well short of nomination.

Conkling and his supporters, including Arthur, had to face the reality that his political popularity had peaked. Although obviously disappointed, he turned to his second goal—keeping his arch-rival James G. Blaine from becoming president. After the fifth ballot, Conkling joined the cabal of other Blaine foes—Morton and Bristow—to thwart Blaine. These powerful, ambitious, and prideful men would not choose one of their number as the nominee, but their determination to prevent a Blaine presidency did lead to their agreeing on Hayes. On the seventh ballot, he gained 384 votes to Blaine's 351. Nominated to run with him was Representative William Wheeler of New York. Both men had solid reputations for integrity.[13]

The Democratic convention met in St. Louis a few days later during June 27–29. Tilden's strength was evident, although on the first ballot his 403½ votes were short of the 492 required. Well back in second place with 133½ votes was Governor Thomas Hendricks of Indiana, a former member of both the House and the Senate. On the second ballot, Tilden secured the nomination, and Hendricks was chosen as his running mate. Democratic optimism was higher than it had been since the summer of 1864 prior to Sherman's military victories in Georgia.[14]

Both parties, reacting to the scandals of the Grant administration, had nominated governors with clean records, and both platforms supported civil service reform, sound money (although Hendricks personally favored greenbacks), an end to Reconstruction, and limits on immigration from the Orient. They differed on land grants to railroads to spur Western development, with the Republicans supporting the policy and the Democrats opposing it. The Republicans still had the stronger party, but their dominance was threatened by the growing prominence of the scandals of the past eight years. The Democrats had seized control of the House of Representatives in 1874 for the first time since 1856, and Tilden was known as a fighter of corruption in New York. More Southern whites could vote again and few of them had any use for the Republican Party, with a legacy of losing the Civil War and experiencing Reconstruction.

Election day, November 7, appeared to validate both Democratic optimism and Republican worries. Hayes went to bed after midnight believing Tilden had won. The popular vote was solidly Democratic, Tilden winning 4,284,757 votes—fifty-one percent of the total—while Hayes trailed with 4,033,950, or forty-eight percent. Dawn brought a faint hope for Republican victory, however. The results from Florida, Louisiana, and South Carolina—where the Reconstruction regimes continued—were not yet clear. Southern whites, overwhelmingly Democratic, were still barred from control. Also, one of the three Oregon electors—all Republicans—was a postmaster and therefore, as the holder of a federal government post, was not eligible. The Democratic governor appointed a fellow Democrat to replace him. The Republicans challenged this.

From the three Southern states came competing sets of election returns. Since the Republicans still controlled these states, the official results gave all three to Hayes. The Democrats, though, challenged them with their own. To resolve the matter, the Republican Senate and the Democratic House of Representatives established a special fifteen-member electoral commission with five senators (three Republicans and two Democrats), five members of the House (three Democrats and two Republicans), and five Supreme Court justices (two Republicans, two Democrats, and one independent named David Davis). But Davis resigned from the Court to accept election to the Senate as a Democrat and was replaced by another justice, a Republican.

To the surprise of no one, the commission voted eight to seven on each dispute, making Rutherford Hayes president of the United States by one electoral vote. Tilden demonstrated statesmanship by accepting the results, refusing to risk tearing the country apart by prolonging the dispute. In a conciliatory gesture, the Republicans agreed to end Reconstruction by withdrawing the remaining military occupation forces from Florida, South Carolina, and Louisiana. In return, black civil rights were guaranteed. The troops did leave, but before long the promise of civil rights died, followed by many decades of white supremacy. A promise by the Hayes campaign to appoint a Southern Democrat to the cabinet was kept by making David M. Key of Tennessee postmaster general. In addition, the Republicans promised the South educational improvement and railroad development.

A miscalculation by the Democrats, often overlooked, also contributed to Hayes's victory. In this presidential election year, they supported the admission of Colorado as a state, convinced that its three electoral votes would be in their column. They were wrong: Hayes won the state. Without these votes, Hayes could not have won the presidency. It would have been immaterial what the electoral commission decided.[15]

The presidential election of 1876 was only the second in which the leader in the popular vote did not win. In 1824, Andrew Jackson was first in the popular vote but did not secure a majority of electoral votes in a year when four powerful candidates split the vote. As specified by the Constitution, the House of Representatives chose from the top three, and it selected John Quincy Adams, who had come in second in the popular vote. Four years later, Jackson won their rematch.

CHAPTER 5

Clash with Hayes

P resident Hayes determined to make the most of the single term to
which he had limited himself. Devoted to the cause of honest government, he looked askance at the Port of New York collector's office, which
epitomized the spoils system. Also attracting the attention of reformers
were the custom houses in Boston, Philadelphia, Baltimore, New
Orleans, and San Francisco—all of them tainted by lax administration,
padded salaries, inflated employment rolls, and bribery, in addition to
collecting money from employees for Republican Party coffers, which
were contributions they made if they wanted to keep their jobs.[1] A growing demand for honesty in government was aiding Hayes and was causing headaches for the Conkling-Arthur organization. Secretary of the
Treasury John Sherman, whose department was responsible for these
custom houses, made the administration's view clear in a letter to Arthur
on May 28, 1877:

> The President properly lays great stress on excluding from a
> purely business office active participation in party politics.
> Naturally, in a government like ours, other things being equal,

those will be preferred who sympathize with the party in power; but persons in office ought not to be expected to serve their party to the neglect of official duty, or to promote the interests of particular candidates, or to interfere with the free course of popular opinion, or to run caucuses or conventions. Such activity of officeholders is offensive to the great mass of the people who hold no office, and gives rise to complaints and irritation. If any have been appointed for political reasons, without regard to their efficiency, now is a good time to get rid of them.[2]

The administration's intent here seemed clear, but relations between Hayes and the New York machine would not be smooth.

Hayes's preference for merit-based civil service, which he believed to be more honest and efficient, brought him into conflict with machine politicians such as Roscoe Conkling. Hayes had no particular quarrel with Arthur, but he was part of the Conkling organization and therefore was unacceptable. The Port of New York was a target of the administration because it controlled so much trade, employed so many people, and generated so much revenue. At first, there was the rather naïve hope that Arthur and Alonzo Cornell, the naval officer of customs for the port, would make everything easy by resigning. When they did not, Hayes suspended them and appointed Theodore Roosevelt, father of the future president, to Arthur's position and L. Bradford Prince to Cornell's. Conkling, still wielding considerable power, saw to it that the Senate defeated the nominations.[3] But Hayes did not back down, continuing to attack the pair as part of a corrupt machine that had to be removed to bring businesslike and nonpartisan operations to the port.

Cracks were starting to form in Conkling's position. The weakness of the Republican Party after the 1876 presidential election mess made his overbearing personality less intimidating. The Democrats retained the control of the House of Representatives, which they had captured in 1874 for the first time since 1856, and in the 1878 midterm election they added the Senate. Conkling's machine in New York was weaker now, and his power in the Senate was starting to fade. He still would be important in the 1880 campaign, but that year marked the end of the Conkling era. In February 1879, Edwin A. Merritt was confirmed as Arthur's replacement, and Cornell's deputy, Silas W. Burt, replaced him. Neither Merritt nor Burt was a Conkling man.[4]

Arthur returned to his law practice, having turned down Secretary of the Treasury Sherman's offer to arrange for him to get the consulship in Paris in return for his resigning quietly as collector. In just over one year, Arthur's rise to the presidency would begin, but for now his political prospects were uncertain, as were those of Roscoe Conkling. His machine, battered but still powerful, was determined to regain its former dominance. The hopes of Conkling and Arthur were buoyed by the approaching end of the Hayes administration. The machine enjoyed a brief Indian summer with the 1879 victory of Alonzo Cornell in the New York gubernatorial race. Now 1880 and another presidential election opened new opportunities for both the Conkling organization and for Arthur personally.

But 1880 first opened for Arthur with the greatest personal tragedy of his life. On January 10, Nell caught a cold while waiting for a carriage after a concert in New York City. It developed into pneumonia, complicated by her not having a strong heart. Arthur was in Albany at the time working to influence the legislature. He rushed to her side, but she was sedated by the time he arrived and did not fully regain consciousness before dying about twenty-four hours later. The New York Assembly passed a resolution of sympathy and adjourned. The political and social leaders of the city turned out for the funeral, along with representatives from both houses of the legislature. Though Arthur loved her deeply, he had frequently been absent from her, caught up in political activity and the attendant social whirl. Remorse worsened the grief, although strength rooted in faith lightened the burden. In her memory, Arthur later contributed a stained glass window in St. John's Episcopal Church across from the White House. It was on the south side of the church so that he could see it from his White House rooms.[5]

On a somewhat lighter note was the contretemps arising after Arthur became president from his having fresh flowers placed daily beside the photograph of a woman. Since so many people love romantic intrigue, the flowers stirred rumors that the president had a new woman in his life. The rumors were squelched when the truth came out that this was a picture of Nell and the flowers were in remembrance of her. There would be no new romance in Arthur's life.

CHAPTER 6

Up to Second Place

I n June, the Republicans convened in Chicago. The way looked clear for Grant, who had been out of office during the Hayes years, to push aside the two-term tradition dating back to George Washington and serve again as president. He was the favorite of the "Stalwarts," the element of the party dominated by Roscoe Conkling, who nominated him in a rousing speech that thrilled most of the delegates.

The idea of another term for Grant was vigorously opposed by the "Half-Breeds," those calling for more reform than their opponents and concerned about the Grant administration's reputation for corruption. Leading them were James G. Blaine of Maine, a senator and former Speaker of the House, and the less important but still powerful John Sherman of Ohio, a former (and future) senator and currently the secretary of the treasury. These men had presidential ambitions of their own, which surely contributed to their opposition to a third term for Grant. Heading the Sherman forces was James A. Garfield of Ohio, the leader of the Republican minority in the House of Representatives, who shortly before the convention had been elected as a United States senator. Despite these differences, the two Republican factions were not deeply divided philosophically. This intraparty divide was the product of the competing ambitions of Conkling and Blaine.

Once the balloting began, it became evident that this would be one of the most contentious conventions in the party's history. Several powerful and experienced leaders were determined to succeed Hayes. Grant was not campaigning openly, but he would readily accept the call for a third term. Blaine and Sherman had risen near the top, had run before, and were powerfully ambitious as another presidential election year opened. A few steps below them, looking hopefully for any faltering by the leaders, were Senator George Edmunds of Vermont; Senator William Windom of Minnesota; Elihu Washburne, briefly secretary of state in Grant's first term before serving as the minister to France under Grant; and Garfield, although Garfield maintained that he supported Sherman.

The first ballot confirmed how seriously divided the party was. Grant led with 304 votes, short of the 379 needed for nomination. Blaine was close behind him with 284, followed by Sherman with 93. Edmunds, Washburne, and Windom trailed, having a combined total of seventy-five votes. The lines were drawn sharply between Grant's supporters and those convinced that his nomination would sink the Republicans in November.

A division in the anti-Grant camp prolonged the contest through the rest of the day and twenty-seven more roll calls. By the end of this exhausting process, little had changed at the top: Grant was first with 307 votes, followed by Blaine with 279, and Sherman with 91.[1] As the second day of balloting began, several Edmunds and Windom votes moved to Sherman, but there was no major shift, and the Sherman total stagnated at 116. But after the end of the thirty-fourth ballot, sixteen votes shifted from Washburne to Garfield, ostensibly a Sherman supporter who until then had garnered only a stray vote at best. On the next ballot, Garfield went over the top, defeating Grant 399 to 306.[2] Blaine and Sherman agreed in their opposition to Grant, but neither man could stand the thought of supporting the other. They could live with a Garfield presidency.

To placate the still powerful Grant wing of the party, the victors offered it the vice presidential nomination. Conkling was not interested in a number-two post, and many of the party leaders didn't want him anyway. He had failed badly at coalition building at the convention, his bullying making enemies for Grant and his parliamentary maneuvers on behalf of the former president falling short. When the convention passed by a vote of 716 to 3 a call for all delegates to pledge support for the nominee, Conkling tried in vain to have the three no-voters, all from West Virginia, expelled, further weakening his standing as a party leader.[3]

The Garfield organization, recognizing the need for a New York Stalwart on the ticket, offered the vice presidential nomination to Representative Levi Morton of New York. He declined and they turned to Arthur, the most prominent Stalwart available. Conkling, pessimistic about the ticket's chances in November and perhaps disgruntled at his own declining fortunes, advised Arthur to reject the offer. But Arthur, recognizing that his old patron's power was receding, demonstrated his independence and responded, "Senator Conkling, I shall accept the nomination and I shall carry with me the majority of the delegation."[4] At this, Conkling stomped out of the room.

Arthur was endorsed by the New York delegation and nominated by the convention, easily defeating Washburne 468 to 193. There were only minor cracks in party discipline. The spat between Conkling and Arthur was alleviated by Conkling's hope that his help for Garfield in a close election could turn the tide for his political standing, as well as by Conkling's affection for Arthur and Arthur's personal charm. This rapprochement took place during a fishing and camping trip in mid-July to the Thousand Islands in northern New York. Shortly after, Conkling wrote, "Gen[era]l Arthur's constant effort was to make every body else happy. No wonder we all like him."[5] Although they were close, Conkling had seen a new Arthur—one who might not remain his subordinate. If that were to happen, the old relationship would be over.

Later in June, the Democrats, their hopes buoyed by the problems of the last two Republican administrations and their own success in

JAMES A. GARFIELD
REPUBLICAN CANDIDATE FOR PRESIDENT

CHESTER A. ARTHUR
REPUBLICAN CANDIDATE FOR VICE PRESIDENT

The Republican ticket of 1880
Courtesy of the Library of Congress

recent congressional elections, met in Cincinnati to select their ticket. Party leaders believed that by nominating Winfield Scott Hancock they could replicate the Republicans' success with Grant. Both were West Point graduates and had achieved fame as generals in the Civil War—Grant at a higher level, to be sure, although Hancock had demonstrated courage under fire and excellent command skills. As military governor of Louisiana and Texas after the war, Hancock favored an expeditious return of civilian rule to the Southern states—a position that put him at cross purposes with the Radical Republicans. He was moved, at his own request, to a command in the Dakota Territory and then to the Atlantic division. Hancock's running mate in 1880 would be William H. English of Indiana, a wealthy banker and former member of the U.S. House.

Since 1880 was expected to be the Democrats' year, however, Hancock's path to the nomination would not be unchallenged. A number of prominent party members saw this as their year of destiny. Senator

Thomas Bayard of Delaware, later secretary of state in the first Cleveland administration, made the second of his three unsuccessful bids for the nomination. He was joined by Henry B. Payne, an Ohio attorney and businessman who had served one term in the U.S. House, and Senator Allen G. Thurman of Ohio, who had lost the governorship to Hayes in 1867. These men had impressive backgrounds, but Hancock's glamour overshadowed them, and he was nominated on the second ballot.

Nominated for vice president by acclamation on the first ballot was William H. English, a former speaker of the Indiana House of Representatives and four-term U.S. representative. He then became a successful banker before reentering politics as the 1880 election neared. English took aim at the vice presidency or, at least, a cabinet position. His wealth and his past political success in Indiana made him attractive to a party hoping for a win after the narrow loss of the presidency four years previously. With a war hero and a rich banker as their ticket, the Democrats were optimistic that victory would be theirs.

The campaign of 1880 was perhaps less exciting than those of the recent past and of the near future. There was little personal vitriol and few differences of policy. Both parties supported sound money and opposed centralizing power in Washington. The one important difference was on trade policy. Democrats believed that low tariffs kept prices down, while Republicans were convinced that higher tariffs protected American businesses and jobs. Each party believed it had the right formula.

The results on November 2 were as close as expected. The Garfield-Arthur ticket narrowly won the popular vote, 4,454,416 (48.3 percent) to 4,449,952 (48.2 percent), and each ticket carried nineteen states. The Republican states were more populous, however, and Garfield won the electoral vote 214 to 155. The reconciliation of Arthur and Conkling allowed Garfield to carry New York by twenty thousand votes out of 1.1 million cast. Had New York gone for Hancock, he would have been elected 190 to 179. Arthur, still mourning the loss of Nell earlier in the year, had masterminded the campaign in the state, showing great energy

Republican campaign poster, 1880
Courtesy of the Library of Congress

and skillfully keeping the feuding factions focused more on Republican victory than on wounded feelings. Although his personal interests were obviously advanced by his becoming vice president, the transformation of Arthur from a machine politician to a leader motivated by higher considerations had begun. The Republicans regained control of the House of Representatives and tied the Democrats in the Senate. The voter turn-out of 78.4 percent testified to the level of civic-mindedness of the time.[6]

To the left of the Republicans and the Democrats, the Greenback Labor Party entered a ticket for the second time, having first competed in 1876. Advocating unbacked paper money, the party had won fourteen House seats in 1878 and looked forward to further progress in 1880, nominating James Weaver of Iowa for president and Benjamin Chambers of Texas for vice president. They did reasonably well in the general election for a recently started party, attracting 308,578 votes, 3.3 percent of the total cast.

For the first time, Chester Arthur was a figure of national prominence, achieving what he thought was the capstone of his career. A few months later, when his succession to the presidency completed one of the most astounding rises in the history of American government, he would evince an unexpected determination to govern as president of all the people rather than as a machine politician.

Garfield was busy during the weeks between the election and his inauguration on March 4 putting together an administration that would govern the country effectively and keep the Republican Party united—no easy task. Although the philosophical and policy differences between the Half Breeds and the Stalwarts were by no means too wide to be bridged, the bruised egos of key Stalwarts made reconciliation difficult. In particular, Roscoe Conkling was seething, still stung by the defeat of Grant at the convention and by the independence displayed by Arthur in accepting the vice presidential nomination over his opposition. The proud Conkling could feel the foundations of his power crumbling in the Republican Party, the Senate, and the state of New York. After meeting with him at Elmira during the campaign, Garfield sized him up in a letter: "Conkling is very strong, a great fighter, inspired more by his hates than his loves; desires and has followers rather than friends.... In his long service he has done little constructive work."[7]

Yet Conkling was still a man to be reckoned with as the new president assembled his administration. During the campaign, the factions had papered over their differences, because unless the Republicans won, nobody gained anything. The new administration wanted Conkling's support, but his bitter enemy James G. Blaine had been chosen as secretary of state, a position then second only to the president in power and prestige. Garfield and Blaine had entered the House of Representatives together in 1863, and over the years they and their families had become friendly. Garfield now asked from Blaine a pledge that he would not run for president in 1884. Friendly or not, Garfield had no intention of promoting a man who might challenge him in four years. Blaine agreed, asking in return that his rival, Secretary of the Treasury John Sherman, not remain in the cabinet. Sherman was happy to oblige, since a Senate seat from Ohio was open and his for the taking.[8] After a few weeks of maneuvering and scheming, the rest of the cabinet would emerge, but not until another chapter in the always fascinating politics of New York unfolded.

In January, the New York legislature met to select a successor for Senator Francis Kernan, a Democrat, who had lost his bid for reelection. The Republican majority was split between three Conkling men—Levi Morton, Richard Crowley, and Thomas Platt. The growing anti-Conkling Half-Breed faction did not control a majority but did have an opening at least to poke the Stalwarts in the eye and weaken their position. They rallied behind Chauncey Depew, a successful attorney who strongly opposed Conkling. Deadlock ensued as no candidate could gain a majority. The president pro tempore of the Senate, William H. Robertson, a Conkling opponent, offered the Half-Breed votes to Crowley if he would agree to vote for the president's nominees who needed Senate confirmation. Arthur, reconciled with Conkling and again working for his interests, stepped in and killed the deal. Platt then was offered the same opportunity. More ambitious and independent than Crowley, Platt accepted, agreeing to support the administration's nominees. He then won the election fifty-five to forty-one.[9]

In February, two hundred of New York's political, business, and social elite gathered at Delmonico's restaurant. Present were such luminaries as John Jacob Astor, J. P. Morgan, Henry Ward Beecher, Thomas Platt, Thurlow Weed, and Robert Todd Lincoln. Neither Blaine nor Conkling attended. After three hours of eating, drinking, and conviviality, former president Grant spoke briefly and introduced former senator Stephen Dorsey, who had served under him in the Civil War and now was secretary of the Republican National Committee. Dorsey in turn introduced Arthur, who was greeted with enthusiastic applause.

After a few serious comments, Arthur resumed the evening's lighthearted tone, commenting that he would not discuss details of the campaign, especially in reference to Dorsey's activities in Indiana, because reporters were present. He observed, "Indiana was really, I suppose, a Democratic state. It had always been put down in the box as a State that might be carried by close and careful organization and a good deal of—" Arthur hesitated as if he were trying to find the right word. The audience entered into the gaiety, shouting "soap," a slang word for vote-buying. Arthur then repeated that he would not get into any further explanations because of the reporters.[10]

It is not clear whether Arthur's remarks to this friendly audience were purely in jest. Perhaps he divulged some truth at this happy get-together of successful New York Stalwarts. He did ignore the criticisms directed at him. At this stage, Arthur still was the New York machine politician—not a man stealing government revenue, but by no means the paragon of the virtuous public servant. His incipient independence from the New York machine had not progressed very far. E. L. Godkin, the editor of the *Nation*, had written of Arthur after he was nominated for vice president that "there is no place in which his powers of mischief will be so small as in the vice presidency."[11]

Before taking the oath of office as vice president, Arthur briefly addressed the Senate:

Senators: I come as your presiding officer with genuine solicitude, remembering my inexperience in parliamentary proceedings. I cannot forget how important, intricate, and often embarrassing are the duties of the chair. On the threshold of our official association, I invoke that courtesy and kindness with which you have been wont to aid your presiding officer. I shall need your constant encouragement and support, and I rely with confidence upon your lenient judgment of any errors into which I may fall. In return, be assured of my earnest purpose to administer your rules in a spirit of absolute fairness, to treat every Senator at all times with that courtesy and just consideration due to the representatives of equal States, and to do my part, as assuredly each of you will do yours, to maintain the order, decorum, and dignity of the Senate. I trust that the official and personal relations upon which we are now entering will be marked with mutual confidence and regard, and that all our obligations will be so fulfilled as to redound to our own honor, to the glory of our common country, and the prosperity of all its people. I am now ready to take the oath of office prescribed by the Constitution.[12]

The tall, well-dressed Arthur made a favorable impression with his commanding presence and self-effacing words.

Garfield determined to form a cabinet reflecting both professional ability and political reality. The premier spot, secretary of state, went to James G. Blaine, still a powerful force in the party. For secretary of the treasury, Garfield chose Senator William Windom of Minnesota, who would serve also under Arthur and Benjamin Harrison. In making this choice, the president once more thwarted Conkling, who had pushed Levi Morton for the position. The secretary of war's position went to Robert Todd Lincoln, the former president's son and an able lawyer who brought the dual advantages of his name and the support of the Stalwarts. The new attorney general, Wayne MacVeagh of Pennsylvania, had supported Garfield at the convention and had ties to the Stalwarts. Thomas Jones, postmaster of New York City, joined the cabinet as postmaster general. A Conkling Stalwart, he did have a reputation for honesty and ability. Senator and former governor Samuel J. Kirkwood of Iowa became secretary of the interior in a nod to the farm states. Judge William H. Hunt of Louisiana, in a gesture to the South, was picked as secretary of the navy.

During the weeks before he was shot, Garfield continued his feud with Conkling, winning Senate confirmation for William H. Robertson as collector of the Port of New York—Arthur's old fiefdom. Conkling's failure to block the Senate action showed clearly that his days of dominating New York were over. Arthur tried to block Robertson, arguing that his confirmation would be a blow to New York Republicans. Garfield countered that this need not be true, that this was a matter that the New York party could solve.[13] Arthur blamed Garfield for not being "square, nor honorable, nor truthful with Conkling."[14] This conflict between Garfield and Arthur, the president and the vice president, is startling. Obviously Arthur had not yet moved very far from his Stalwart machine roots. This round went to Garfield. It is interesting to ponder how well Garfield would have brought the warring factions together had he not been shot.

Conkling, stung by his recent defeats and feeling his grip on power slipping, tried a desperate gamble. He resigned his Senate seat, persuading his colleague Thomas Platt to do the same. The plan was that the New York legislature then would reelect them, strengthening their prestige and power, but the scheme failed. Aware of the weakness of the Conkling machine, the legislature selected two other men, leaving Conkling and Platt out of office.[15] Platt, younger than Conkling and more nimble politically, would make a comeback, but the political career of the older, more rigid Conkling, who had made too many enemies, was over.

The four months that elapsed between Garfield's inauguration on March 4 and his shooting on July 2 were marked by a plague of patronage demands and the emergence of the Star Route scandal, which involved defrauding the government on rural mail delivery contracts and would carry over into the Arthur administration.

After the shooting of the president, while the vice president maintained a decidedly low profile, the Garfield wing of the Republican Party confronted the appalling prospect of Garfield's dying and being succeeded by Arthur. On July 3, after learning of the shooting, former president Rutherford B. Hayes reflected, "The death of the President at this time would be a national calamity whose consequences we can not now confidently conjecture. Arthur for President! Conkling the power behind the throne, superior to the throne! The Republican Party divided and defeated."[16] Hayes never would fully recognize the changes in Arthur as president. Nearly three years later, he wrote that Arthur "is a Stalwart except when driven into reform positions by a public sentiment which he dare not resist."[17]

This demeaning view of Arthur was shared by the editors of the *New York Times*, who wrote after the president was wounded, "Active politicians, uncompromising partisans, have held before the office of Vice-President of the United States, but no holder of that office has ever made it so plainly subordinate to his self-interest as a politician and his narrowness as a partisan."[18] It would be difficult to express a more unfavorable evaluation of someone on the verge of becoming president of the United States. Such was the reality with which he had to deal as he stepped into the breach.

Once he received official word of Garfield's death, Arthur moved quickly to ensure continuity. John Brady, a state judge, was summoned to Arthur's New York home and administered the oath of office just a few hours later at a quarter past two in the morning. Later that morning, Arthur took a special train to Elberon, where he joined Lucretia Garfield and members of the cabinet to accompany Garfield's body back to Washington. Two days after, on September 22, Chief Justice Morrison Waite administered the oath at an official ceremony in Washington before key members of Congress and former presidents Ulysses Grant and Rutherford Hayes. After the oath, Arthur kissed the Bible and reminded the country:

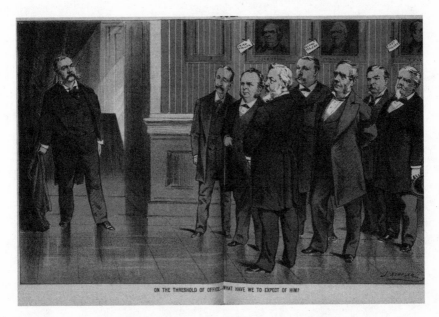

ON THE THRESHOLD OF OFFICE—WHAT HAVE WE TO EXPECT OF HIM?

"On the Threshold of Office—What Have We to Expect of Him?"
Courtesy of the Library of Congress

Men may die, but the fabrics of our free institutions remain unshaken. No higher or more assuring proof could exist of the strength and permanence of popular government than the fact that, though the chosen of the people be struck down, his constitutional successor is peacefully installed without shock or strain except the sorrow which mourns the bereavement.[19]

The growth of Arthur was becoming clear.

The new president, it should be noted, had by this time contracted Bright's disease, now called nephritis, a kidney ailment that causes nausea, mental depression, and indolence. Until dialysis and kidney transplants became available, it was a death sentence. Arthur may have already begun to experience the early symptoms of the disease—he would know he had it by 1882—but it was not yet evident to those in his administration. His endurance would decline over the last months of his presidency, and those closest to him would know of his illness, but the general public would learn of it only after his death. Considering the debilitating effects of Bright's disease, Arthur deserves particular praise for how well he handled the burdens of office.

CHAPTER 7

The New President

On September 22, Arthur offered words of reassurance to the shaken nation, reminding Americans of the extraordinary stability of their government:

> For the fourth time the officer elected by the people and ordained by the Constitution to fill a vacancy so created is called to assume the Executive chair. The wisdom of our fathers, foreseeing even the most dire possibilities, made sure that the Government should never be imperiled because of the uncertainty of human life. Men may die, but the fabrics of our free institutions remain unshaken. No higher or more assuring proof could exist of the strength and permanence of popular government than the fact that though the chosen of the people be struck down his constitutional successor is peacefully installed without shock or strain except the sorrow which mourns the bereavement.[1]

In a proclamation issued the same day, Arthur designated September 26 a day of national mourning, calling for Americans to gather that day in their places of worship and "[t]here to render alike their tribute of sorrowful submission to the will of Almighty God and of reverence and love for the memory and character of our late Chief Magistrate."[2]

In these statements, Arthur reminded the people that God is sovereign, that the country would remain strong, and that the new president's hand was on the tiller.

The depth of Arthur's spiritual convictions is not clear. His letters to Nell quoted earlier give some insight, but the career of a New York machine politician was not conducive to spiritual growth. Perhaps the death of Nell and the magnitude of his new responsibilities revived the deeper, better side of Arthur. No woman replaced her in his personal life.

New York Stalwarts rejoiced that one of their own was president. Others feared that the country had been saddled with a corrupt and self-serving administration. Both would be mistaken. Arthur's first priority was to ensure stability and continuity by persuading the members of the cabinet to remain. His success was limited, but those who departed were replaced by able men.

Secretary of State Blaine, now freed from his pledge to Garfield not to run for president in 1884, agreed to stay in the cabinet until December, when Congress would convene. Since he and Arthur represented opposing wings of the Republican Party and most likely would be rivals for the party's 1884 presidential nomination, this resignation, which was in each man's interest, was no surprise. Frederick T. Frelinghuysen of New Jersey, a Rutgers graduate, attorney, and U.S. senator, succeeded him and continued the expansion of U.S. influence, especially in the Americas.

Secretary of the Treasury William Windom of New Jersey would not serve under a Stalwart president. He resigned shortly after Garfield died to run for a U.S. Senate seat. Arthur offered the post to Governor Edwin Morgan of New York, who declined because of poor health, and the position was eventually filled by another New York Stalwart, Charles Folger, chief justice of the New York Court of Appeals.

Secretary of War Robert Todd Lincoln was the only member of the Garfield cabinet to serve throughout the Arthur years. A successful attorney, he later served as ambassador (at the time the title was "minister")[3] to the United Kingdom and as president of the Pullman Car Company. There was some interest in his running for president, but he never entered the fray.

Attorney General Wayne MacVeagh was another Garfield appointee who refused to stay on now that a Stalwart was president. He was replaced by Benjamin Brewster, a Princeton graduate who had been the attorney general of Pennsylvania.

The incumbent secretary of the navy was William Hunt of Louisiana, who had opposed secession but held a non-combat position in the Confederate army. He recognized the poor state of the U.S. Navy and took initial steps to reverse the decline. Arthur favored building up the navy, but he had someone else in mind to lead the charge. In April 1882, Hunt resigned to become the American ambassador to Russia. The new secretary of the navy was William E. Chandler of New Hampshire. A Harvard Law School graduate who had been speaker of the New Hampshire House of Representatives and judge advocate general of the Navy Department, he later would be elected to the U.S. Senate. Chandler would play a pivotal role in the United States' becoming a naval world power.

Postmaster General Thomas L. James of New York was another who refused to remain in the cabinet under Arthur. Senator Timothy O. Howe, a Wisconsin Stalwart, replaced him but died the next year.

Secretary of the Interior Samuel J. Kirkwood of Iowa, another Arthur opponent, resigned early in 1883 and was replaced by Senator Henry M. Teller of Colorado, a Stalwart who supported homesteaders in the West in their struggles with cattlemen and speculators. He also pushed vocational education programs for Indians to further their integration into American life.

Considering that Arthur took over an administration assembled by the Garfield wing of the party and that he had to replace almost the entire cabinet, he did well asserting control and forming an administration that capably handled its responsibilities and was loyal to him. He passed this key test of leadership—picking good subordinates who he ensured did their jobs well.

Arthur's cronies and associates from his old machine days quickly discovered that the presidency was changing him. When they entered his office, put up their feet on his desk, and addressed him as "Chet," as they were accustomed to doing, Arthur brought them up short, told them to take their feet off his desk, and to address him as "Mr. President."[4] His insistence on decorum was a sign not of pride, but of his understanding that he was president of the United States first and only secondarily their friend. Once that was established, he could relax, but he would not forget that the office must come first.

In October, Conkling traveled to Washington to confer with Arthur. They met in the home of Senator John P. Jones of Nevada, where Arthur had his office and his residence while the White House was being renovated. There are no official records of the meeting, but it lasted for several hours and became heated. Conkling apparently had hoped that his former protégé would be the means for him to regain influence, if not power, and that his law practice, at least, would be stimulated. It is likely that Conkling, as part of his return to power, sought the removal of William Robertson as collector of the New York custom house. Arthur, determined to be president of all, not just a Stalwart machine leader, refused, provoking an outburst of vitriol from Conkling. Arthur later said, "For the Vice-Presidency I was indebted to Mr. Conkling, but for the Presidency of the United States my debt is to the Almighty."[5]

Conkling, still capable of mounting a powerful challenge to Arthur, had to be treated carefully. In January 1882, Arthur nominated him for the U.S. Supreme Court. The Senate confirmed him by a vote of thirty-nine to twelve, but Conkling, for reasons that are not clear, refused to assume the position.[6] Perhaps he still had hopes for his political resurrection. Perhaps a seat on the Supreme Court did not seem as important as it would seem in later generations. Perhaps he was by this time aware of how far he had fallen and was in a grumpy, self-pitying mood. At any rate, there would be no rapprochement between them. For the remaining

Arthur and Conkling: "The Original Political Dude Out-Duded"
Courtesy of the Library of Congress

years of his life, Conkling's law practice in New York City would flourish, but his political significance was no more.

Arthur did choose two men for the Supreme Court who were confirmed and served. Horace Gray had been chief justice of the Massachusetts Supreme Judicial Court. Garfield had nominated him for the court, but was shot before the Senate confirmed him. Honoring Garfield's intention, Arthur renewed the nomination. An economic and social conservative, Gray served on the court for twenty years. One of his most consequential decisions was in *United States v. Wong Kim Ark*, holding that a child born on U.S. soil is a full citizen of this country.[7] His law clerks included the future justice Louis Brandeis.

Arthur's other appointment to the Supreme Court was Samuel Blatchford of New York, a federal court judge with fifteen years on the bench. His name went to the Senate within two weeks of Conkling's refusal. Blatchford was known as an expert in admiralty law.[8] Neither he nor Gray is ranked among the greatest Supreme Court justices, but each was a solid professional and a credit to the American judiciary. They both died while active members of the Court—Blatchford in 1893 and Gray in 1902.

During these years, as is true today, judicial ability and experience were considerations in choosing justices, but then as now new members of the Supreme Court had philosophical and political beliefs which certainly entered into their selection. The hope always is that when deciding cases, constitutional principles will prevail over partisan considerations.

Arthur not only had to repopulate his cabinet, fill judicial vacancies, and deal with his disgruntled old boss Conkling, but also had to move into a new home, and he was appalled at its rundown condition. During Grant's and Hayes's terms, little had been done to maintain the White House, let alone correct its deterioration. The septic system was decayed and stinking. Whitewash was peeling off the kitchen walls and falling into pots on the stove.[9] Arguing that action was overdue, Arthur stepped in decisively.

He briefly considered calling for a new structure, but the claims of history overcame practicality and he settled for renovation. The renowned interior designer Louis Comfort Tiffany of New York was engaged for the project. Twenty-four wagonloads of furniture and other household items were removed and sold at a public auction, partially defraying the cost. On April 15, 1882, five thousand people gathered for the event. The building was repainted, new wallpaper was installed, and new furniture brought in. After three months, Arthur moved into what was again an impressive executive mansion. A more thorough restoration would have to wait for Theodore Roosevelt, who made the interior more consistent with the Federal-period exterior.[10]

On December 7, 1881, Arthur moved into the White House. His younger sister, Mary, who was married to John McElroy, agreed to fill the social role of the first lady four months of the year. Her oldest daughter, May, was a companion for Arthur's ten-year-old daughter, Nell, born November 21, 1871, whom he protected from public scrutiny. During these presidential years, his son Chester Alan Arthur II was a student at Princeton. White House social events during the Arthur years were convivial, but dignified and elegant. At formal dinners the Marine Corps band played classical music. The renowned opera singers Adelina Patti and Christine Nilsson, a friend of Arthur's late wife, performed there, as well.[11]

There were limits, though, to Arthur's affability at social events—especially when guests brought their political causes with them. When a crusading prohibitionist criticized his serving alcoholic beverages at his White House events, in contrast to the "dry" years of Rutherford Hayes and his wife, "Lemonade Lucy," he responded formally but acidly, "Madam, I may be president of the United States, but my private life is nobody's damned business."[12] This rebuff expressed both his determination to retain his private life and his opposition to the growing temperance movement, which coincided with the movement for women's votes. At this time, the top national leaders in both major parties were not on board.

Arthur did not favor extending the vote to women. When the most prominent suffragette, Susan B. Anthony, and one hundred members of the National Woman Suffrage Association met with him at the White House, Anthony assured the president that his prospects for winning a full term of his own in 1884 would be much enhanced if he supported amending the Constitution so that women could vote. According to a report of the encounter:

> This little speech of Miss Anthony rather nonplussed the President, who, after some hesitation, made a reply, which was of a non-committal character. He, however, in a pleasant manner, formally welcomed the ladies, and said he felt certain that, as the ladies were earnest and determined, they would secure what they ought to have. Not to be outwitted by this flank movement, Miss Anthony persisted in asking, "Ought women not to have full equality and political rights?" To this Mr. Arthur replied, "We should probably differ upon the details of that question."
>
> [Back at the suffrage convention], Miss Anthony opened the afternoon session, with the hall two-thirds full of ladies, by telling something of what had happened.... "I asked him," said Miss Anthony, "if he did not think women ought to have the same rights and privileges as men. He answered—well; I don't think anybody could tell which way it was he answered, but it was very polite."
>
> Miss Anthony's clever way of expressing the President's non-committal responses excited much laughter in the audience.[13]

Arthur, always a gentleman with the ladies, would not, though, endorse this crusade. Although Wyoming had voted in 1869 to enfranchise women, total victory for the suffragettes with the nineteenth amendment still lay years in the future.

The advocates of women's suffrage confronted not only the inertia of men who disliked change, but also those who objected to their cause in principle. Among these was the renowned historian Francis Parkman (1823–1893), known for *The Oregon Trail* and for his multi-volume *France and England in North America*. *Montcalm and Wolfe*, perhaps the best-known book in the series, came out in 1884, the year Parkman published his remarks about women. Parkman's historical writings were brilliantly vivid. His contentions as to why women should not vote were certainly vivid, as well. He argued:

> Whatever liberty the best civilization may accord to women, they must always be subject to restrictions unknown to the other sex, and they can never dispense with the protecting influences which society throws about them. A man, in lonely places, has nothing to lose but life and property; and he has nerve and muscles to defend them. He is free to go whither he pleases, and run what risks he pleases. Without a radical change in human nature, of which the world has never given the faintest sign, women cannot be equally emancipated.... Everybody knows that the physical and mental constitution of woman is more delicate than in the other sex.
>
> Woman suffrage must have one of two effects. If, as many of its advocates complain, women are subservient to men, and do nothing but what they desire, then woman suffrage will have no other result than to increase the power of the other sex; if, on the other hand, women vote as they see fit, without regarding their husbands, then unhappy marriages will be multiplied and divorces redoubled. We cannot afford to add to the elements of domestic unhappiness.
>
> To give women a thorough and wholesome training both of body and mind...[is] in the way of normal and healthy development: but to plunge them into politics, where they are not needed and for which they are unfit, would be scarcely more a movement of progress than to force them to bear arms and fight....[14]

If Parkman's fears were excessive, so too were the promises that if women had the vote, societal conditions would improve, saloons and gambling halls would be regulated, and the level of morality would be raised. The suffragette leader Elizabeth Cady Stanton (1815–1902) boasted, "As mothers of the race, there is a spiritual insight, a divine creative power that belongs to women."[15]

There is some truth in both positions, but each is simplistic and misses the key point that both sexes cause their share of societal problems. The solution is an orderly, just society within which people are free to develop their talents without being either advanced or held back because of their sex.

Educational opportunities for women did grow impressively during the middle and later years of the nineteenth century. Oberlin College, which opened its doors in 1833, and Antioch College, which did so in 1852, were coed from their foundation. In addition, a number of women's colleges started during these years, beginning with Vassar College in 1865. By 1889, it was joined by Mount Holyoke, Wellesley, Smith, Radcliffe (affiliated with Harvard), Bryn Mawr, and Barnard (affiliated with Columbia).[16] And women across the country were being admitted to previously all-male colleges and universities.

Also during these years, professional opportunities opened more for women. In 1870, the suffragettes Victoria Woodhull and her sister, Tennie C. Claflin, opened a brokerage business in New York City as the first women to enter this profession. Their ability and a good relationship with the tycoon Cornelius Vanderbilt brought impressive success before they closed their office in 1872 to focus on politics.[17]

Just beginning her rise to prominence as Arthur's presidency ended was Nellie Bly (1864–1922), the most prominent of the early women journalists. Christened Elizabeth Jane Cochran, she was nicknamed "Pink" because of her cheek color. At the age of fifteen, she entered the State Normal School at Indiana, Pennsylvania, to prepare for a teaching career. Financial problems forced her to withdraw after one term. Her career in journalism began in January 1885 with the *Pittsburgh Dispatch*, where "Nellie Bly" was assigned to her as a pen name, a common practice then for women in the field.[18]

Bly's fame grew when she moved up to the *New York World* and persuaded the paper to support her attempt, inspired by Jules Verne's extraordinarily popular novel *Around the World in Eighty Days*, to circumnavigate the earth in less time than the fictional Phileas Fogg required. This she did, completing the journey in seventy-two days, six hours, eleven minutes, and fourteen seconds.[19] Her fame was now assured and continued to grow.

An altogether different controversy involving women arose out of Utah. Settled by Latter-day Saints led by Brigham Young in 1849, the territory had been seeking statehood for twenty years, but the Mormon practice of polygamy undermined its cause. In his first annual message on December 6, 1881, Arthur referred to polygamy as an "odious crime so revolting to the moral and religious sense of Christendom."[20] He continued that Congress and the president have "the duty of arraying against this barbarous system all the power which under the Constitution and the law they can wield for its destruction."[21] He discussed the dismissal by the U.S. Supreme Court of a polygamy conviction on the grounds that secrecy in Utah concerning marriage records made getting evidence for a conviction too difficult. Arthur called for Congress to enact legislation permitting testimony by a woman married to a man charged with bigamy. He further admonished Congress to pass legislation requiring that anyone performing marriages in U.S. territories be required to file certificates of those marriages with the territorial supreme court.[22] Now in the 1880s, federal courts stepped up the enforcement of anti-polygamy laws.

The Mormon leaders understood that polygamy would keep Utah from statehood, so in 1890, Wilford Woodruff, the president of their church, called for its abandonment. Five years later, Utah adopted a state constitution prohibiting polygamy, and it was admitted to the union in 1896. A few years later in 1904, the Mormon church formally repudiated the practice.

Arthur's leadership on this issue was easy, for few were willing to defend polygamy. Other battles would be considerably more difficult.

Congress came back into session on December 5, 1881, sitting until August 8 of the next year. Both houses had narrow Republican majorities, and the party's leadership was less than distinguished. A further liability for the Republicans was Arthur's own weak base of support. He belonged to neither the dominant Half-Breed faction nor the Stalwarts, although the latter saw him as one of them early on. Under these circumstances, few people would have been surprised had Arthur simply gone along with what the key members of his faction wanted. But the Stalwart hopes that he would promote their interests turned to ashes as Arthur gave further proof that he was rising above his background in the party machine. Roscoe Conkling had encountered a new Arthur; soon others would, as well.

On October 26, 1881, the "Gunfight at the O.K. Corral" in Tombstone, Arizona Territory, made celebrities of Wyatt Earp, his brothers Virgil and Morgan, and John "Doc" Holliday. These men, especially Wyatt Earp and Holliday, became national figures thanks to the ongoing American fascination with the frontier, centering especially on Indian fighters, lawmen, and explorers. As early as the second half of the seventeenth century, Benjamin Church of the Plymouth Colony made a name for himself in campaigns against the Indians. Daniel Boone, Davy Crockett, and John Frémont later became heroes because of their frontier exploits. In the last three decades of the nineteenth century, George Armstrong Custer and William "Buffalo Bill" Cody won lasting fame, as did Bartholemew William Barclay "Bat" Masterson and James Butler "Wild Bill" Hickok.

In the Arizona Territory of 1881, the dividing line between lawmen and criminals often was shadowy. The Earp brothers did hold law enforcement positions, but there were times in their careers when they seemed to stray outside the law. Little could be said, though, for their opponents that October day—the brothers Ike and Billy Clanton and the brothers Tom and Frank McLaury. After the exchange of gunfire, Billy Clanton and Tom McLaury were dead while Virgil and Morgan Earp and Doc Holliday were wounded. A few months later, Morgan Earp would be assassinated, and Virgil Earp would retire as a lawman after suffering a serious gunshot wound. In 1887, Doc Holliday died of tuberculosis. Wyatt continued in law enforcement and various business interests, eventually retiring to southern California, where he became friendly with people in the rapidly growing film industry, among them Charlie

Chaplin, Tom Mix, William S. Hart, and a young John Wayne. He was the focal point of a number of books, but no film of his life was made prior to his death in 1929. Interest in Earp was revived by movies in the 1930s, 1940s, and 1950s when he was played by Randolph Scott, Henry Fonda, and Burt Lancaster, and on television from 1955 to 1961 when the role was Hugh O'Brian's.[23] More recent notable portrayals of Earp were by Kurt Russell in *Tombstone* and Kevin Costner in *Wyatt Earp*, both of which were released in the mid-1990s.

Returning now to the 1880s, the need for law and stability in Arizona led the governor of the territory, Frederick A. Tritle, to request help from the federal government. He had been appointed to his post by Arthur on February 6, 1882. Now that the call for assistance had been made officially, Arthur responded affirmatively. He asserted the right of the president to order the use of military force in the territory if necessary to ensure order. He closed his decree with the call for voluntary compliance and a warning:

> Now, therefore, I, Chester A. Arthur, President of the United States, do hereby admonish all good citizens of the United States and especially of the Territory of Arizona against siding, countenancing, abetting or taking part in any such unlawful proceedings; and I do hereby warn all persons engaged in or connection with said obstruction of the laws to disperse and retire peaceably to their respective abodes on or before noon of the 5th day of May.[24]

The proclamation was on target. The army stayed in the background as a protection against Indians and as a last resort should chaos prevail. It didn't. Even if Arthur did not have to use military force, his willingness to do so promoted peace. Order and justice came to the West with the growing recognition that prosperity would come only as productive people with families moved and settled. Mining, cattle ranching, and farming—thanks to irrigation—brought that prosperity.

The United States Army, which had become one of the most power-ful in the world by the end of the Civil War, had declined rapidly as the country reverted to its standard opposition to large standing armies. On May 1, 1865, men numbering 1,034,064 were in uniform. By November 15, a total of 800,963 men had been discharged and had returned to their homes. The next July, Congress authorized 54,302 officers and men. That figure was reduced in 1869 to 45,000. In 1875, a further reduction established a force of 27,442—a size that would remain about the same until 1898 and the war with Spain.[25]

As support for the regular army faded, the national guard partially compensated. The National Guard Association was formed in 1879 to support the growth and improvement of this part-time force. Unless called into federal service, the national guard units were under the command of state governors. Those who feared both an outbreak of the revolutionary violence that had afflicted other countries and a powerful national gov-ernment were reassured. The national guard also provided a rallying point for men seeking fraternity and the satisfaction of duty fulfilled.

During these years between the Civil War and the Spanish-American War, the regular army found itself outside the mainstream of national life. There was little danger of invasion from Canada or Mexico or of enemy landings on our coasts. Through the Arthur years, campaigns against hostile Indians continued, primarily in the Southwest, but few Americans felt menaced and the number of soldiers involved was small, so most people were not intensely interested in military matters.

Rather than giving way to discouragement, the regulars became more professional, more determined. West Point still educated capable officers, and the small regular force would provide a solid nucleus for the rapid expansion of 1898 and for later national emergencies. Arthur's reforms, limited though they were, will be discussed later.

CHAPTER 8

Arthur and Race

In his first year in the White House, Arthur confronted the question of how to deal with American Indians, a quandary dating back to the first European settlements in North America. By the time Arthur became president, the Indian wars were almost over. In New Mexico, Arizona, and across the border into Mexico, the Apaches maintained their independence and fighting continued. Although there were tensions between the United States and Mexico, the two countries cooperated against the common danger from the Apaches. Conflict flared throughout Arthur's presidency, ending shortly after he left office in 1885.[1]

The last of the prominent Indians to follow the path of war against the expansion of the United States was the leader of the Chiricahua Apaches, Goyahkla, better known by the name the Mexicans gave him—Geronimo. His courage and determination were recognized by Americans who fought him, as were his viciousness and vile temper. In 1858, Mexican soldiers had killed his wife, his children, and his mother.[2] For decades, he fought both Americans and Mexicans, moving back and forth across a national border that meant nothing to him.

By 1881, attempts to settle the Apaches on reservations had been somewhat successful. But war flared again that year as Geronimo led off the reservation a force determined to assert their independence. For several years, they raided and killed in both countries, evading the numerically superior forces sent against them. The spread of civilized order, though, was too powerful to be halted. When pressed hard, the Apaches agreed to return to the reservation before becoming restive and renewing the war. Finally on September 4, 1886, Geronimo and his band surrendered and were exiled to Florida. They later were given reservation land in Oklahoma, where Geronimo lived until 1909.[3] Although there would be tensions and a clash at Wounded Knee, South Dakota, in December 1890, the Indian wars were over and a chapter of American history had closed.

There remained the dispute concerning whether the Indian tribes should be seen as defeated foreign nationals, their people kept on reservations, or whether they now should be seen as Americans and integrated. In his first annual message, Arthur announced that he opposed treating them as "separate nationalities" and "encouraging them to live a savage life, undisturbed by any earnest and well-directed efforts to bring them under the influences of civilization."[4]

Arthur believed that the Indians should be integrated into the mainstream of American life: "For the success of the efforts now making to introduce among Indians the customs and pursuits of civilized life and gradually to absorb them into the mass of our citizens, sharing their rights and holden to their responsibilities, there is imperative need for legislative action."[5]

He wanted to see educational opportunities extended for them to promote this integration. In 1881, the Carlisle Indian Industrial School opened in Pennsylvania, and in 1882 similar programs started in Hampton, Virginia, and Forest Grove, Oregon. However, the Indians' progress from an educational and technological base far less advanced than that of most other Americans, was slow.

Drawing much the same conclusion was Carl Schurz, secretary of the interior under Hayes, who earlier in 1881 had written:

The greatest danger hanging over the Indian race arises from the fact that, with their large and valuable territorial possessions which are lying waste, they stand in the way of what is commonly called "the development of the country."

A rational Indian policy will make it its principal object to avert that danger from the red men, by doing what will be most beneficial to them, as well as to the whole people: namely by harmonizing the habits, occupations, and interests of the Indians with that "development of the country."

To accomplish this object, it is of pressing necessity to set the Indians to work, to educate their youth of both sexes, to make them small proprietors of land, with the right of individual ownership under the protection of the law, and to induce them to make that part of their lands which they do not need for cultivation, profitable to themselves in the only possible way, by selling it at a just rate of compensation, thus opening it to general settlement and enterprise.[6]

This policy was to be only partially successful. The controversy has continued over whether to foster integration of Indians into the mainstream of American life or to focus more on reservations and ethnic separateness. Headaches continue to the present as policy makers struggle to reconcile those who want to see the Indians integrated into the mainstream of American culture and those who insist on seeing the Indian reservations as semi-independent political entities.

The most prominent Indian leader during the second half of the nineteenth century calling for their integration into American life was Quanah Parker (c. 1850–1911). His father was Peta Nocona, a prominent Comanche war chief. His mother was a white woman, Cynthia Ann Parker, who had been captured in 1836 at nine years of age. The date of Quanah's birth is not certain. He said of himself, "From the best information I have I was born about 1850 on Elk Creek just below the Wichita Mountains."[7] By that time, Cynthia Parker was assimilated as a Comanche. About ten years later, she was recaptured in a raid by Texas Rangers while Nocona and Quanah were away hunting. Cynthia was restored to her family but never really reassimilated into American life. She died young in her brother's home in Texas. Nocona died two or three years later.[8]

In his mid-teens now, Quanah, a strapping six-footer, was a skilled warrior and was soon to be war chief of the Quahadas, one of the twelve or so bands of Comanche warriors. He proved himself as a brave and capable combat leader in the vain attempt to halt the westward movement of the United States. Finally in 1876, Quanah's band surrendered near Fort Sill, Oklahoma, among the last of the Comanche to abandon war. Then he led his people on a new path.

Since the Indians' effort to stop by military means the westward movement of the United States had failed, Parker recognized that the Comanche—and Indians in general—faced only three alternatives: assimilation, permanent subjugation, or annihilation. He led the way down the first trail, encouraging his people to gain education, to farm, to raise cattle. He himself became a successful rancher with a two-story home near Cache, Oklahoma. His constructive, successful leadership led to his becoming principal chief of the Comanche in 1890.[9]

There were, though, some areas of Parker's personal life which remained traditionally Indian. He respected Christian missionaries and supported their ministries among his people, but did not become a Christian himself, continuing to practice the peyote ritual. He continued also as a polygamist, having eight wives—although only two in his later years—by whom he fathered twenty-five children. Furthermore, he retained his braided hair—Indian fashion. Parker understood the public relations advantages of his being a renowned warrior and played that role for parades and county fairs, riding his horse in the full regalia of a Comanche chief. Under normal circumstances, he dressed as a regular American businessman.[10]

Parker was a pivotal figure in the history of American Indians. His biographer Bill Neeley writes, "Not only did Quanah pass within the span of a single lifetime from a Stone Age warrior to a statesman in the age of the Industrial Revolution, but he accepted the challenge and responsibility of leading the whole Comanche tribe on the difficult road to their new existence."[11]

Parker was not alone in his determination to integrate Indians into the United States. Also prominent in this movement was Susette La Flesche (1854–1903), also known by her Indian name, Bright Eyes. An educated young woman of the Ponca tribe, born near present-day Omaha, Nebraska, she brought suit in federal court to secure her people's freedom as American citizens. The U.S. attorney assigned to the case argued that Indians were not citizens and therefore could not sue the government. Judge Elmer Dundy ruled in 1879 for the Indians in *United States ex rel. Standing Bear v. Crook*, holding that "an Indian is a Person within the meaning of the laws of the United States" and is entitled to sue for habeas corpus "where he is restrained of liberty in violation of the Constitution or laws of the United States." Indians, he wrote, have an "inalienable right to life, liberty, and the pursuit of happiness."[12]

The Hayes administration considered appealing the decision but decided to accept it. Most press opinion and public opinion supported the ruling.

Literature also was used to promote the improvement of the status of Indians. Most significant was Helen Hunt Jackson (1830–1885), whose *A Century of Dishonor* (1881) called for better treatment of the Indians. The year after its publication, President Arthur appointed her to investigate the treatment of mission Indians in California. Disappointed that her book had not sparked more interest, Jackson now turned to fiction, which she believed would reach more people. Her best-known book, *Ramona* (1883), tells the story of a mixed-race woman raised by an aristocratic Spanish family in California. After her Indian husband is murdered, she is barred from testifying at the trial of the killer because he is white.[13] Four movies have been based on the novel.

The Indians of the American West were among the finest light cavalry in military history, ranking with the Scythians, the Huns, and the Cossacks. The Indian wars had kept sharp the skills developed by young officers during the Civil War, men who now had risen to the top of their profession and would lead the American forces fighting Spain in Cuba, Puerto Rico, and the Philippines in 1898. For example, commanding that last campaign against Geronimo was Nelson A. Miles (1839–1925), a dashing cavalry leader in the Civil War and a major general at twenty-five. Reduced in rank to colonel in the peacetime army, he had to start the climb again. He later would be the commanding general of the United States Army during the Spanish-American War, taking charge personally of the Puerto Rican invasion.

Another young Civil War general who later successfully led army units against the Indians was George Crook (1828–1890). He undoubtedly was the best combined Indian scholar and Indian fighter. A West Point graduate, the crusty, self-confident Crook was a skillful and successful cavalry leader during the Civil War, finishing the war as a brevet major general. His Indian policy called for defeating them militarily and then integrating them into American society. In 1883, he defeated Geronimo and the Chiricahua Apaches, made peace with them, and secured their return to the reservation assigned them. In 1885, the Apaches bolted from the reservation and went back on the warpath, prompting criticism of Crook's policy and his resignation. Miles now was assigned command and secured the final victory. Wesley Merritt (1834–1910) also had been a major general during the Civil War while still in his twenties, served in Indian campaigns, and commanded the American seizure of the Philippines.

A still younger generation of soldiers gained useful experience in the Indian wars. Prominent among them was John J. Pershing (1860–1948), the commander of the American armies in Europe in World War I. A graduate of West Point, he served in the last campaign against the Apaches, although his unit saw no combat. Other veterans of the Indian campaigns holding high rank during World War I included Hunter Liggett (1857–1935), who led the First Army, and Robert Lee Bullard (1861–1947), his counterpart in the Second Army. For most Americans by the time of Arthur's presidency, Indian wars now were in the pages of history.

European settlers had found the Indians here when they arrived, and the question to be decided as white civilization spread across the continent was whether and how to integrate a once independent people. Blacks, on the other hand, were in America because Europeans had transported them here as slaves. Although there were free blacks in the United States when the country was founded, a few of whom had prospered, most Americans of African ancestry had gained their freedom only with the Union victory in the Civil War. Over the decade and a half between emancipation and Arthur's presidency, progress for them had been real, but slow, and they faced the determined opposition of many.

The Reconstruction policy of barring supporters of the Confederacy from government left control of the Southern states in the hands of blacks, the minority of whites who had remained pro-Union ("scalawags"), and Northerners who had moved into the region to take advantage of opportunities opened up by the Union victory ("carpetbaggers"), and for a few years Southern blacks rose rapidly. Two, in fact, were elected to the United States Senate—Hiram Revels and Blanche Bruce, both from Mississippi. Revels, born free, was chosen to fill out the remaining months of the term to which Jefferson Davis had been elected before the Civil War. Completing the term in 1871, he moved on to be president of Alcorn University, now Alcorn State University. Bruce was elected to a full Senate term in 1874. By the time he completed his term, Southern whites had regained the vote. Solidly in the ranks of the Democratic Party, they ousted Republicans subject to state control, especially black Republicans, who bore a double stigma. Bruce then served in the Garfield and Arthur administrations as register of the United States Treasury.

Senator Ben Tillman of South Carolina exemplified the worst in Southern Democrats by opposing education for blacks and their right to vote. After the Democrats regained control of the South Carolina government in the 1876 election, he crowed, "We shot negroes and stuffed ballot boxes."[14] This was not mere colorful language. Tillman later clarified this policy: "The negro must remain subordinate or be exterminated."[15] In

1881, Tennessee segregated railroad cars and began segregation by law, a policy labeled "Jim Crow" after a minstrel show song which was sung by white performers in blackface. By 1884, the black vote would be down by one-quarter in Mississippi, by one-third in Louisiana, and by one-half in South Carolina.[16]

The end of Reconstruction set back black civil rights in the Southern states. Still, in the thirteen years after Reconstruction ended in 1877, school enrollment and literacy rates for blacks in this country increased by more than forty percent, and real estate ownership by blacks tripled. Colleges and universities for blacks opened—notably Howard, Morehouse, Fisk, and Tuskegee, all of which were located in Southern states where segregation was enforced rigidly. The nation's first public high school for blacks was Dunbar High School in Washington, D.C., founded by William Syphax, a free black born in 1826. He exhorted his fellow blacks to support education, which would train young people to work hard with discipline and respect for others. Syphax preferred to employ black teachers, but race was not the paramount consideration; their educational and professional qualifications at least had to equal those of white teachers.[17] By the end of the century, Dunbar students scored higher in city-wide tests than did students in white high schools. In addition, attendance generally was better and tardiness rates lower than in the other high schools.[18] In addition to the emphasis on academic excellence, students were introduced to culture through, for example, music and the stage. Syphax was determined to prove that allegations of inherent black inferiority were a canard and that given opportunity his people could achieve as much as those of European ancestry could.

Outside the South, institutions slowly integrated. Black doctors, lawyers, and teachers increased in number. But most of these advances were in the context of the black community. Rarely did these professionals deal with an integrated clientele. Equality of opportunity still lay in the future.

Also set back during these years was the integration of major league baseball. The first black player had been Moses Fleetwood Walker

(1857–1924), who in 1884 became a catcher with the Toledo Blue Stockings of the American Association, then a major league. Walker, born in Ohio and the son of a minister and physician, had attended Oberlin College, where he was the first black in intercollegiate baseball. He went on to the University of Michigan Law School before turning professional. A good catcher but a mediocre hitter, he ended his career in the sport in 1890. Pressure built, especially from Southern teams, to bar blacks from major league baseball, and Walker was the last black major leaguer until Jackie Robinson joined the Brooklyn Dodgers in 1947, ending the color barrier permanently.[19]

Arthur confronted a racial controversy shortly after he assumed the presidency. Lieutenant Henry Ossian Flipper was the seventh black to attend West Point and the first to graduate. Born a slave in 1856, he had earned the respect of many at the academy, including General William Tecumseh Sherman, for his "pluck and gentlemanly qualities," as the *New York Herald* phrased it.[20] From 1879 to 1880, he saw action against the Apaches with the Tenth Cavalry, one of two black cavalry regiments. Flipper was the first black officer to command a unit of regulars. Earlier in 1881, he had been court martialed on what probably were trumped-up charges. He was found innocent of embezzling commissary funds but guilty of "conduct unbecoming an officer and gentleman" and dishonorably discharged. Flipper maintained his innocence. The judge advocate general and Secretary of War Robert Todd Lincoln recommended against his discharge, but Arthur rejected their advice and declined to reinstate Flipper. Why he did so is not clear. As is evident from his past defense of blacks, racial prejudice cannot explain his failure to act. Perhaps he wanted to limit the number of controversies so early in his administration. Whatever the reason, this certainly was not his finest hour.

Flipper moved on to an impressive career in mining and surveying, wrote several books, and served as the first black editor of an American newspaper not in the black community—the *Nogales Sunday Herald*. He also returned to government service, holding important posts with the Interior Department in Alaska and Washington. He died in 1940. In

1977, West Point established the Henry O. Flipper Memorial Award for "leadership, self-discipline, and perseverance in the face of unusual difficulties while a cadet,"[21] a well-deserved honor.

Johnson Chesnut Whittaker, born a slave, was Flipper's roommate at West Point for one year until Flipper graduated and was commissioned. In April 1880, just two months before graduation, Whittaker was found in his room, tied to his bed, beaten, slashed, and unconscious. The commandant of cadets believed Whittaker had faked the incident to avoid failing a philosophy course. He demanded a court of inquiry. Public opinion supported Whittaker, as did President Hayes, who appointed as head of the inquiry General Oliver O. Howard, a Civil War veteran, former head of the Freedmen's Bureau, and a strong supporter of black civil rights. Before procedures began, Whittaker was dismissed from West Point for failing the philosophy course.[22]

The court-martial was held from January to June 1881. Whittaker was found guilty, but leniency was recommended. In the fall, the judge advocate general of the army overturned the verdict on a technicality. Then in March 1882, Secretary of War Lincoln invalidated the trial, this time with Arthur's support. Whittaker gave a speech in Buffalo pledging, "With God as my guide, duty as my watchword, I can, I must, and I will win a place in life."[23] He successfully practiced law and taught in South Carolina and later moved to Oklahoma, where he also taught and became a public school principal.

Perhaps the most prominent black man in the latter decades of the nineteenth century was Frederick Douglass, born a slave in Maryland in 1818. Fleeing bondage, he escaped to Massachusetts in 1830. Largely self-educated with assistance from supportive people who saw his potential, he founded a newspaper, the *North Star*, in Rochester, New York. He enhanced his reputation with his autobiography, *Narrative of the Life of Frederick Douglass*, published in 1845 and followed by expanded versions in 1855 and in 1881. He became a popular speaker, supporter of emancipation, and a prominent Republican. Hayes appointed Douglass marshal for the District of Columbia, and in 1881 Garfield named him recorder of deeds for the same jurisdiction, a post he would hold throughout Arthur's presidency. On April 16, 1883, Douglass addressed an audience that had gathered in Washington, D.C., to commemorate the twenty-first anniversary of Lincoln's Emancipation Proclamation. He was optimistic that progress for black Americans would come as they gained education and skills and as the general population recognized their contributions. He and most blacks saw the Republican Party as the pathway for their political rise.[24]

Douglass discussed "[t]hree different solutions to [the problem of American blacks that] have been given and adopted by different classes of the American people. 1. Colonization of Africa; 2. Extinction through poverty, disease and death. 3. Assimilation and unification with the great body of the American people."[25] Rather obviously, Douglass considered the third alternative best both for blacks and for the country as a whole.

Two black Americans who later advocated sharply different paths for progress were Booker T. Washington (1856–1915) and W. E. B. Du Bois (1868–1963). Washington founded the Tuskegee Normal and Industrial Institution in 1881 to help blacks achieve professional and economic success. Born a slave as the son of a slave woman and a white blacksmith, he graduated in 1875 from Hampton Normal and Agricultural Institute, which had been founded in 1868 by the American Missionary Association to train black teachers. The head of the school and the key influence in its founding, General Samuel Chapman Armstrong, who had commanded black troops during the Civil War, invited Washington back to Hampton in 1879 to speak at commencement and hired him to lead a new night school program for students who had to work all day to afford an education.[26] Washington did well, but his surge to national prominence was just ahead.

In 1881, Alabama established an educational institution at Tuskegee to educate black teachers. General Armstrong was asked for a recommendation for a man to head it, the expectation being that he would be white. Armstrong responded that Washington was the only man he could support for the position, that he was "a very competent capable mulatto, a clear headed, modest, sensible, polite, and thorough teacher and superior man." In conclusion, he characterized Washington as "the best man we ever had here."[27]

There may appear to be an element of condescension in this praise, but that is judging the words from the vantage point of the twenty-first century. Armstrong's evaluation of Washington came only a few years after the ending of slavery and was indicative of substantial progress toward racial justice. Washington believed that the path blacks should take in their rise began with education and economic gains before moving on to political and social advancement.

William Edward Burghardt Du Bois's approach to racial progress diverged sharply from that of Washington. Born shortly after the end of slavery, he entered Fisk University, a black institution in Tennessee, in 1885. He moved on to Harvard University in 1888, enrolling as a junior and graduating cum laude in 1890, then earned his M.A. in 1891 and his Ph.D. in 1895—the first black to do so. Du Bois achieved success as a teacher, starting at Wilberforce University, as an author, and as a political activist. For years, he was a leader in the National Association for the Advancement of Colored People (NAACP), eventually giving up on it and the Democratic Party as not radical enough. His political and philosophical migration culminated in his joining the Communist Party, repudiating his American citizenship, and dying a voluntary exile in Ghana. David Levering Lewis, a biographer only mildly critical of Du Bois, offers this assessment:

> In the course of his long, turbulent career, then, W. E. B. Du Bois attempted every possible solution to the problem of twentieth-century racism—scholarship, propaganda, integration, cultural and economic separation, politics, international communism, expatriation, third-world solidarity.[28]

Though Du Bois's most influential years came after Arthur's presidency, he was the most important counterpoint to Washington's approach to racial improvement. The dispute continues concerning what path blacks should take to rise.

Relations between Arthur and Frederick Douglass were not good, although Douglass continued as recorder of deeds throughout his presidency and into the first term of Grover Cleveland. Douglass castigated Arthur:

> The death of Mr. Garfield placed in the presidential chair Chester A. Arthur, who did nothing to correct the errors of President Hayes, or to arrest the decline and fall of the Republican Party, but, on the contrary, by his self-indulgence, indifference, and neglect of opportunity, allowed the country to drift (like an oarless boat in the rapids) towards the howling chasm of the slave-holding Democracy.[29]

What went wrong between Arthur and Douglass is not clear. The president certainly had no racist proclivities. Perhaps his determination to avoid any hint of favoring the spoils system led him to steer clear of those involved with it, which included Douglass. Yet he wanted no overt break with so prominent a black man. Perhaps Arthur was so involved in other crusades that he chose not to intensify this one. Certainly his declining health during the latter part of his term required him to choose carefully how many conflicts he entered. Still, a certain mystery remains. In summation, the Arthur presidency brought for black Americans neither dramatic progress nor tragic retrogression. Its successes came in other areas.

CHAPTER 9

Taking Charge

In the years after the Civil War, there was a growing revulsion with the political spoils system. Reformers sought a civil service in which hiring would be based on competitive examinations rather than political connections. Positions at the top of the bureaucracy would continue to be political appointments, changing with the results of the latest election. But lower-level positions would constitute an ongoing bureaucracy, staffed by technically skilled professionals whose political convictions, the reformers assumed, would not affect their performance. This would not always be the case. It can be argued that civil service did bring improvement, but no system will work well if honor and ability do not prevail. The key problem was not political appointments, but that those making the appointments were motivated more by their personal gain through corruption than by principles of honesty and efficiency.

The assassination of Garfield gave new impetus to calls for reform. A few weeks after Arthur took office, the *New York Times* observed, "Centers of discussion and agitation are now found in many of the principal

States of the Union, from Massachusetts to California, and there is no doubt that their influence will be felt at the next session of Congress."[1]

The public supported reform, while most political professionals feared it. In 1882, Congress rejected Arthur's call to move on the issue. The president expressed concern that competitive examinations might determine "mere intellectual attainments," but he advocated a central examining board that would determine the qualifications of applicants without resorting to tests and affirmed his willingness to support any reform bill that Congress would pass.[2]

Now that he was president, Arthur was rising above the New York spoils system from which he had emerged, determined to bring about improvements though aware that his lack of a national base of political power limited what he could achieve. Congressional opposition combined with Arthur's weak base and relatively low charisma—he lacked the persuasive powers of a Lincoln or a Theodore Roosevelt—stalled reform until the election results that autumn shook the Republican establishment out of its complacency.

Although the Republicans narrowly won control of the Senate in 1882, they lost badly in House races, falling from a twelve-seat advantage to a seventy-nine-seat deficit. The Republicans also lost the governorship of New York. Arthur's fellow Stalwart, Alonzo Cornell, was running for a second term, but Arthur supported Charles Folger for that office. Hoping to improve Folger's prospects, Arthur had appointed him secretary of the treasury. It was also true that Arthur, knowing both men, believed Folger would be the better governor. Folger won the nomination, but the deposition of Cornell alienated many New York Republicans, who suspected that Arthur was trying to build his own machine. He might have been showing strength and leadership, but his years in the Conkling machine still were remembered.

On the Democratic side, two powerful candidates vied for the gubernatorial nomination, both of whom had served in the U.S. House of Representatives. Roswell P. Flower, a wealthy Wall Street figure, had the support of the upstate party, and Henry Slocum, a general in the Civil

War, was backed by the New York City machine. There was, though, substantial dissatisfaction in Democratic ranks, where it was feared that neither man had the stature nor background to win the support of reform-minded voters—especially those in the Republican Party. Former Governor Samuel Tilden, who had almost won the presidency in 1876, was in declining health but still a force in state politics. His long-time supporter, Daniel J. Manning, was chairman of the state party. They regarded neither Flowers nor Slocum as a strong candidate or likely to be an honest, efficient governor. Grover Cleveland, elected mayor of Buffalo the previous year, was their fresh-faced alternative. He already had established a reputation for honesty, courage, and ability. When the Democratic convention voted in Syracuse on September 21, Cleveland won the nomination on the third ballot.

In the November election, Cleveland defeated Folger 535,318 to 342,646—a crushing margin of fifty-eight to thirty-seven percent.[3] The combination of Cleveland's virtues and resentment of Arthur's intervention doomed Republican chances for victory. This was a setback for Arthur's campaign to control his party, but it was by no means a fatal one. The decline of Roscoe Conkling's power in both the U.S. Senate and in New York opened the door for Arthur's taking control of the state party.

Shaken by the national election results, Republican leaders who had dragged their feet now tried to get out in front of the reform wave rather than being pushed to the side by it. They determined to enact civil service reform in a lame-duck congressional session before the Democratic majority took over. This would keep the Democrats from getting credit for reform and keep in office the Republicans already there.[4] Even such a determined Stalwart supporter of political spoils as Senator John Logan of Illinois felt the heat. A general under Grant and Sherman in the Civil War, Logan was angling for the Republican presidential nomination and wanted to be on the winning side of this popular issue. Members of both parties felt the heat, and the Pendleton Civil Service Reform Act passed in the Senate on December 27 by a margin of thirty-nine to five and passed in the House on January 4, 1883, by 155 to 46.

The legislation was introduced by Senator George H. Pendleton, an Ohio Democrat who previously had failed to interest his fellow senators in reform. Now the changes in the political landscape made his name nationally known, but his stance so alienated party leaders in Ohio that he soon lost his seat. For the moment in 1882–1883, though, his career was at its high point and his name known nationally.

The British civil service system provided the inspiration for the reformers. Qualification for middle-tier and lower-tier positions was to be determined by performance on a competitive examination—not by party loyalty. Retaining office would not be dependent on loyalty to a party or on the success of any particular party at the polls. The Pendleton Act established a three-man commission, appointed by the president and confirmed by the Senate, to oversee the whole apparatus. Until 1956, when Congress specified a six-year term for the commissioners, they held office at the pleasure of the president.[5]

To the pleasant surprise of the reformers, Arthur supported their cause. His choices for commissioner were solid: Dorman B. Eaton, chairman of the short-lived Civil Service Commission during Grant's presidency; John M. Gregory, president of the University of Illinois; and the Democrat Leroy D. Thoman, who earlier had lost an Ohio race for a seat in the U.S. House to William McKinley. About ten percent of federal employees were covered initially by the Pendleton Act.[6] During subsequent years, the reform movement would suffer downtimes, but civil service now was entrenched and would grow from this modest start. By the end of Grover Cleveland's second term in 1897, almost 50 percent of the federal workers were in the system,[7] and when Theodore Roosevelt left office in 1909, the number had grown to 66 percent.[8]

As far as most Americans were concerned, Arthur was on the right side of this issue. The opposition of many professional politicians strengthened his appeal. His term less than half completed and his respect and popularity growing after several key battles, the situation appeared promising for Arthur to secure the 1884 Republican nomination and win a term of his own. He still, though, had to overcome the problem that one wing of the party believed that he had abandoned them and the other saw him as not one of them.

Another contentious matter confronting Arthur in his first year in office was his remission of the sentence imposed on General Fitz John Porter by a general court-martial in January 1863. Porter, a graduate of West Point, commanded the V Corps in the Army of the Potomac under General George McClellan, a Democrat who disagreed with most of Lincoln's war aims, although he did want to see secession ended and the country reunited. Running for president against Lincoln in 1864 as the Democratic nominee, McClellan called for conciliating the Confederate states by not forcing them to abolish slavery if they came back into the Union.[9] Porter supported this policy of opposing the Lincoln administration while stopping short of overt disloyalty.

Porter served ably in McClellan's unsuccessful 1862 Peninsula Campaign to seize Richmond, a failure because of McClellan's excessive caution and Confederate general Robert E. Lee's brilliance. Lincoln pushed McClellan to the edge, placing his hopes on the newly formed Army of Virginia commanded by General John Pope, who had done well in Western operations against the Confederates. Porter commanded his corps under Pope in the Second Battle of Bull Run on August 29–30, 1862, in which he refused to obey an order from Pope to attack, maintaining that Pope was unaware that Longstreet's Confederate corps was on his flank in a position to devastate his force if the ordered attack went forward. Certainly Porter was not the critical factor in the battle; Pope was befuddled and thoroughly out-generaled by Lee, just as McClellan had been.

Some historians have defended Porter's decision as right under the circumstances while others have castigated him for not communicating with Pope. As a result of this defeat, Pope was removed from his command, which was combined with that of McClellan, again the principal Union hope.

Court-martialed for disobedience, disloyalty, and misconduct, Pope was found guilty, dismissed from the military, and excluded from all other government service. Historians still are divided between those who consider

Porter a scapegoat caught in the crossfire between Lincoln and McClellan, and those who condemn him as "pusillanimous," guilty as charged.[10]

Looking back dispassionately, the charges brought against Porter seem unjustified, although a case can be made that his contemptuous words about President Lincoln violated the Articles of War's prohibition of "contemptuous or disrespectful words against the president of the United States" or certain other officials.[11] Certainly Porter, as well as McClellan and others in the army, were guilty of this, but Porter appeared to have been singled out and made an example.

In 1879, Porter's case was reopened, and on January 10, 1883, Arthur ordered the "full remission" of his penalties.[12] All things considered, especially since more than twenty years had passed since the events of 1862 and Lincoln had led the Union to victory, this pardon was justified. The horrors of the Civil War were fading, and Americans had turned to the work of building an industrial and commercial colossus.

In 1883, the Brooklyn Bridge opened, linking the formerly separate cities of Manhattan and Brooklyn, which at the time were the largest and third-largest cities in America. (In 1898, Manhattan, Brooklyn, Queens, the Bronx, and Staten Island would unite as New York City.) An engineering marvel, it was the longest suspension bridge in the world and the first built of steel, stretching 3,579 feet with a main span of 1,595 feet. Towers 275 feet high supported steel cables sixteen inches thick. Construction had begun in 1869 under the leadership of the German-born engineer John A. Roebling, who died following an accident shortly after the work began. His son Washington, an 1857 graduate of Rensselaer Institute and an artillery colonel in the Civil War, stepped in and oversaw the completion of the project. Twenty men died building the bridge, most of them from the bends, contracted from rising too rapidly to the surface after working on the foundation in pressurized compartments below water level. Washington Roebling himself suffered the bends as he rose to the surface one day in 1872. He lived until 1925, although partially crippled, and his wife completed the work with his supervisory help.[13]

The formal opening of the bridge was on May 24, which happened to be Queen Victoria's birthday—a coincidence that provoked fears of

JUNE 2, 1883.   HARPER'S WEEKLY.   341

THE GREAT BRIDGE—PRESIDENT ARTHUR AND HIS PARTY CROSSING THE SUSPENDED HIGHWAY.—Drawn by Schell and Hogan.—[See Page 345.]

"The Great Bridge: President Arthur and His Party Crossing the Suspended Highway"
Courtesy of the Library of Congress

violence from supporters of Irish independence. The *New York Tribune* commented acerbically that "it would be difficult, perhaps impossible, to fix upon a day that did not commemorate something or other unpleasant for Ireland."[14] To ensure that everything went as planned, nine hundred policemen were assigned to maintain order, of whom 150 secured the Fifth Avenue Hotel, where Arthur was staying along with his son, four members of his cabinet, and Governor Grover Cleveland.[15]

Joining the dignitaries for the opening ceremony were Mayor Franklyn Edson of New York and Mayor Seth Low of Brooklyn. They crossed the bridge from Manhattan to Brooklyn. Three hours of prayers, music, and speeches, all by local dignitaries—neither Arthur nor Cleveland was invited to speak—preceded the formal declaration that the bridge was open. The festivities were followed by a reception for the president at the Music Academy in Brooklyn, which went on until ten o'clock that night.

Those present commented that Arthur appeared healthy and animated, clearly enjoying the event, and that when walking across the bridge from Manhattan to Brooklyn, he "trod the pathway with an elastic step."[16] He was careful to keep his medical condition private to avoid the appearance of seeking sympathy and, no doubt, for the sake of political stability. Questions about a presidential vacancy would have been more troubling than usual because there was no vice president. (It was not until 1967 that the Twenty-fifth Amendment to the Constitution provided for the appointment of a new vice president when the office is empty.)

There were, though, more astute observers of Arthur's appearance who noted, as reported in the *New York Herald*, "an unaccustomed pallor to his lips and cheeks."[17] The president's illness kept him at the Fifth Avenue Hotel for a week, the public being reassured that he was suffering from a minor indisposition.

CHAPTER 10

Conflicts Intensify

L abor violence could have been a problem for Arthur, but the worst of it flared after he had left office. The Knights of Labor, founded in 1869, had brought the organized labor movement to prominence. A secret fraternal society as well as a labor organization, it was open to men and women, white and black, skilled and unskilled. Its demands went beyond an eight-hour work day and the prohibition of child labor to include a graduated income tax, the nationalization of railroads and utilities, the abolition of private banks, and the establishment of coopera- tives to oppose private business.[1] At the peak of its power in 1886, membership in the organization hit 729,000, of whom about seventy thousand were women and sixty thousand were black.[2]

President Arthur was by no means ambivalent about the program of the Knights, but the crises they provoked arose when Grover Cleveland was president. The Knights won a victory against Jay Gould's Southwest Railway in 1885, but the next year they lost a rematch against Gould railroad interests. Far more damaging, however, was their involvement in the Haymarket Square violence in Chicago in 1886. Most of the public now rejected the Knights, repulsed by their violence and radical beliefs.

As is common, their decline led to internal squabbles that accelerated that decline. They were pushed further toward oblivion by the American Federation of Labor, founded in 1886 and led by Samuel Gompers, which pushed for higher wages and better working conditions within the market economy. Gompers and the new labor movement rejected socialism, violence, and the destruction of property as the paths to progress.

Immigration

In 1882, his first full year as president, Arthur engaged Congress in two emotionally charged confrontations. The first was over a bill to exclude further Chinese immigration for twenty years. The second was the Rivers and Harbors Act, a classic piece of pork-barrel legislation.

The United States was always a land of immigrants, but by the middle and later years of the nineteenth century, an increasing number of immigrants were not of British origin. They came from Ireland, Germany, Italy, and Eastern Europe,[3] and integration was difficult for the first generation. Most now came from countries with languages other than English, and those who were Roman Catholic or Jewish often clashed with segments of the American Protestant majority. The all too common suspicion of newcomers was exacerbated by their willingness to work for less than those already here. But many in succeeding generations rose professionally and economically, overcoming prejudice, joining the mainstream, and lessening societal tensions.

The Chinese entering the United States from 1850 to 1882 encountered the same problems as those from European nations, intensified by racial and sharper cultural differences. The main, but not exclusive, destination of Chinese immigrants was California. From 1850 to 1882, more than 322,000 Chinese moved to the United States. The first ones were prosperous merchants, skilled artisans, hotel and restaurant owners, and fishermen, but the building of the transcontinental railroad after the Civil War attracted a substantial number of lower-skilled Chinese. The Central Pacific, the western end of the project, employed fourteen thousand workers, ninety percent of whom were Chinese.[4] By 1870, more than half the miners in Oregon and Idaho and a quarter of those in California and Washington were Chinese.[5] In 1873, Chinese workers made most of the shoes and boots produced in San Francisco, and by 1886 the Chinese accounted for almost ninety percent of the farm workers in California.[6]

American workers resented the competition, and Gompers's American Federation of Labor refused membership to ethnic Chinese. Prejudice crossed economic and class lines—although then, as later, those in favor of an open door were often interested in low-cost labor. Of course, many Americans favored, as a matter of principle, taking in those seeking freedom and opportunity.

The Chinese Exclusion Act of 1882 reflected prejudice more than a reasoned decision about how many immigrants the United States could prudently admit. It prohibited further Chinese immigration for twenty years and required Chinese entering the United States to have a passport in English describing the bearer and countersigned by an American consular official in China.[7] In his April 4 veto message, Arthur condemned the bill, writing that "a nation is justified in repudiating its treaty obligations [referring to earlier agreements with China] only when they are in conflict with great paramount interests" and that "resorting to the supreme right of refusal to comply with them" is only a last resort.[8]

Congress could not override Arthur's veto. A compromise bill was passed reducing the twenty-year prohibition to ten years, but leaving the rest of the bill intact. Arthur considered this as much as he could get from Congress and signed it on May 6. He did not have the political power base to challenge further the national and congressional sentiment opposing additional Chinese immigration. As he grew into the presidency, he demonstrated more combativeness, such as when he vetoed the Rivers and Harbors Act and pushed civil service reform in the teeth of bipartisan congressional opposition. The Chinese Exclusion Act was renewed in 1892 for another ten years, then in 1902 for an indefinite time. Finally, it was repealed once and for all in 1943.

Concerning both Chinese immigration and how to handle the Indians, Arthur advocated policies more enlightened than most political leaders of his time. The difficulties of welcoming persons of different ethnicities and religions while maintaining the commonalities that unify countries are a continuing challenge.

Pork-Barrel Legislation

Bills such as the Rivers and Harbors Act of 1882 routinely passed through both houses of Congress. Arthur approved of a number of the act's projects, but he was appalled at the burgeoning overall cost and the purely local nature of many of the projects funded. His veto message of August 1, 1882, warned of the corrupting influence of such wasteful pork-barrel measures:

> Appropriations of this nature, to be devoted purely to local objects, tend to an increase in number and in amount. As the citizens of one State find that money, to raise which they in common with the whole country are taxed, is to be expended for local improvements in another State, they demand similar benefits for themselves, and it is not unnatural that they should seek to indemnify themselves for such use of the public funds by securing appropriations for similar improvements in their own neighborhood. Thus as the bill becomes more objectionable it secures more support. This result is invariable and necessarily follows a neglect to observe the constitutional limitations imposed upon the lawmaking power.

The appropriations for river and harbor improvements have, under the influences to which I have alluded, increased year by year out of proportion to the progress of the country—great as that has been. In 1870, the aggregate appropriation was $3,975,900; in 1875, $6,648,517.50;

and in 1881, $11, 451,000; while by the present act there is appropriated $18,743,875.

The extravagant expenditure of public money is an evil not to be measured by the value of that money to the people who are taxed for it. They sustain a greater injury in the demoralizing effect produced upon those who are entrusted with official duty through all the ramifications of government.[9]

It is not unusual for politicians to lament the misuse of the taxpayers' money, but it is a rare officeholder who is willing to antagonize his own party and the highly motivated voters who stand to benefit from a program that would be paid for by someone else.

As expected, Congress overrode Arthur's veto, but his stand against pork-barrel projects earned him widespread praise for being both right and courageous. Considerably less impressed was the historian H. Wayne Morgan, who doubted Arthur's sincerity. In his view, "The President probably expected [the override] and was no doubt grandstanding anyway...."[10] Arthur's motive in vetoing the Rivers and Harbors bill cannot be known with certainty, but his overall record as president gives us more reason to suppose that his veto message was sincere than to join Morgan in his cynicism.

This was not the first battle over government spending, nor would it be the last. The next president, Grover Cleveland, phrased the principle powerfully and succinctly in one of his veto messages: "Though the people support the Government, the Government should not support the people."[11] Arthur did not explain his veto as pithily, but his convictions on the question were as firm as his successor's.

Sound Money

Monetary policy is a perennial source of division in American politics. Increasing the amount of money in circulation is a constant temptation for politicians looking for a way to keep the good times rolling without worrying about taxation, spending, and deficits. During the second half of the nineteenth century, sound money men like Arthur, who understood the necessity of maintaining confidence in the medium of exchange, confronted the powerful and seductive voices who promised prosperity simply by inflating the money supply. Many favored printing more paper currency without worrying about backing for it—a tactic tried during the Revolutionary War and the Civil War but abandoned when the crisis passed and sound economic thinking returned. The economist Thomas Sowell explains the issue incisively and succinctly:

> The big problem with money created by the government is that those who run the government always face the temptation to create more money and spend it. Whether among ancient kings or modern politicians, this has happened again and again over the centuries, leading to inflation and many economic and social problems that flow from inflation. For this reason, many countries have preferred using gold, silver, or some other material that is inherently limited in supply, as money. It is a way of depriving governments of the power to expand the money supply to inflationary levels.[12]

When the Civil War ended in 1865, there was a powerful sentiment to restore the sound dollar and to remove unbacked paper money from circulation, though some peddled the deceptively simple nostrum that merely increasing the amount of money in circulation and spending it would bring about prosperity. These two sides would compete vigorously until the sound dollar forces won with the Gold Standard Act of 1900, a victory that would last a few decades before giving way in stages to the counterattack of the unbacked paper forces. The lawyer and financier James Rickards, an advocate of the gold standard, wrote that the classical gold standard that dominated the world economy from 1870 to 1914 "was hugely successful and was associated with a period of price stability, high real growth, and great invention."[13]

In the 1870s, proponents of inflation were calling for a more subtle policy, arguing that the unlimited minting of silver coins would increase prosperity. Since silver has intrinsic value, this course of action, although inflationary, was less harmful than printing unbacked paper. Many people did not understand that increasing the amount of money in circulation regardless of economic growth decreases the value of the dollar and leads to higher prices. The key consideration is not the amount of money people have, but the value of it.

The inflationists suffered a setback in 1870 when the U.S. Supreme Court ruled in *Hepburn v. Griswold* that making greenbacks (unbacked paper) legal tender violated article 1, section 8 of the Constitution, which gives Congress the power "to coin money," and section 10, which prohibits states from making "anything but gold and silver coin a tender in payment of debts...." Republicans were not yet broadly committed to sound money, and the Grant administration, opposing the ruling in *Hepburn*, soon filled two vacancies on the Supreme Court with justices who favored the administration's position. The following year, in *Knox v. Lee*, the Court reversed *Hepburn*, ruling that unbacked paper as legal tender did not violate the Constitution.[14]

The sound money forces were dealt a major blow in 1878 when Congress, over the veto of President Hayes, passed the Bland-Allison Act, mandating that the government purchase and mint between two million and four million dollars' worth of silver each month.[15] The Hayes administration and its five successors purchased the minimum amount, mitigating somewhat the inflationary pressure. But the conflict continued, sharply dividing the country.

Proponents of inflation scored a more substantial victory in 1890 when the Republican-controlled Congress passed the Sherman Silver Purchase Act, which required the government to purchase 4.5 million ounces of silver every month, roughly doubling what Bland-Allison required. The silver was paid for with paper money, which could be redeemed for either gold or silver. As more people understood that the value of silver now would diminish, more paper was redeemed for gold, causing a serious drop in the government's gold supply.[16]

Economic uncertainty hurt the Republicans in the midterm elections of 1890. The Democrats gained two Senate seats, although the Republicans still held control. The change in the House of Representatives, though, was dramatic—the Democrats surged from 159 seats to 235, and the Republicans sank from 166 to 88. Two years later in a rematch of the presidential election of 1888, Benjamin Harrison lost his bid for a second term and Grover Cleveland returned to the White House with both houses of Congress in Democratic hands. Just after he began his term on March 5, the country was hit by the ravages of an economic depression—the "Panic of 1893." Its impact and the leadership of Cleveland led to the repeal of the Sherman Silver Purchase Act in 1893. In 1900, during William McKinley's presidency, the United States formally adopted the gold standard.[17] It remained in place until Franklin Delano Roosevelt ended the formal gold standard in 1933. In 1971, Richard Nixon cut the last tie to gold when he stopped foreign governments from exchanging their dollars for gold.[18]

As president, Arthur supported the gold standard, although the most critical decisions about it were made before and after his term in office. Prior to 1880, most of his political involvement was on the state and local levels, but no attraction to the silverite or greenback positions crops up in his record. In fact, in his fourth annual message to Congress on December 1, 1884, he called for Congress immediately to stop the coinage of silver and the issuance of silver certificates.[19] Once again, Arthur took a firm stand on a contentious issue but was overshadowed by presidents before him and after him during whose administrations the matter became more contentious.

Post Office Scandals

During Garfield's short time in the White House, it became clear that supervision of Post Office Department contracts had gone awry and that a serious public scandal was brewing. Congress subsidized mail delivery to rural areas in the South and the West—called star routes—because those awarded contracts committed to deliver the mail with "certainty, celerity, and security." Those words were marked on the postal clerks' registers by three stars.[20] Contracts for these 2,225 routes were awarded on the basis of favoritism to supporters and friends of the administration. Investigations in the 1870s had accomplished little. Garfield's incapacity after his wounding impeded a solution. Shortly after settling in as president, Arthur directed his attorney general, Benjamin Brewster, to clean out the rot. The process began.

On March 4, 1882, a grand jury indicted nine men, the most prominent of whom were Senator Stephen Dorsey of Arkansas, Second Assistant Postmaster General Thomas J. Brady, and Montfort C. Rerdell, a clerk of Dorsey's. They were charged with a conspiracy centering on nineteen mail routes on which payments had shot from $4,135 to $448,671.[21]

The trial finally began on June 1 and dragged on until September 15. Arthur's past friendship with men such as Dorsey and Brady led them to expect his support, and reformers assumed that he opposed cleaning up government. Rerdell and one other defendant were found guilty, one was acquitted, and the jury was hung on the others. Because of irregularities, the judge set aside the verdict and ordered a new trial.[22]

The second trial dragged on from December 7 until June 14, 1883. The *New York Times* credited the prosecution with making a solidly convincing case. Once again, the lawyers for the defense endeavored to confuse the jury and to wear it down. They succeeded, and all the defendants were found not guilty. Allegations of jury tampering, though probably true, were never proved. The *New York Times* faulted the jury:

> A great part of the evidence must have been beyond their comprehension. It was certainly unfortunate that in the greatest conspiracy case ever tried in this country the proof was laid before men who could not understand it because of their

stupidity and lack of common education, who were fuddled with whiskey, or who yielded, unconsciously perhaps, to arguments not made in court.[23]

Arthur was wounded by suspicions that he still was a Stalwart and had favored the defendants. There was no doubt, however, that he deserved credit for supporting the prosecutions which ended the scandals and saved the government money.

Krakatoa

The year 1883 also saw one of the most destructive volcanic eruptions in recorded history—that of Krakatoa on the island of the same name in the strait between Java and Sumatra in the Dutch East Indies (now Indonesia). This volcano might have erupted in A.D. 416 and 535 and probably did in 1680. Although people living in the region understood the reality of volcanic dangers, they had not experienced an eruption of Krakatoa, and a complacent unreality suffused their thinking; they believed it was sleeping peacefully. Then in May, tremors were felt and a lighthouse at the southeastern entrance to the Sunda Strait, which separates Java and Sumatra, shifted on its foundation. Still, few people imagined that catastrophe was just below the horizon. Through May, June, July, and into August, periodic tremors and a rising plume of steam raised the level of concern, though few anticipated what would come.[24]

On Sunday afternoon and evening, August 26, eruptions became more frequent and of greater magnitude. Early the next morning a series of four gigantic explosions began. More than thirty-six thousand people died, most killed by tsunami waves up to 130 feet high. The explosions were heard three thousand miles away. The rock, ash, pumice, and dust hurled into the atmosphere produced dramatically red sunsets for three years and dropped average world temperatures by about one degree Fahrenheit over the next five years.[25]

Tariffs

Until the income tax was imposed by constitutional amendment in 1913, tariffs on imported goods were the primary source of federal revenue. From 1791 to 1815, the duties on imports were about 12.6 percent of their value. After the War of 1812, pressure for increased protection of American businesses led to higher tariff rates, and by 1832, the level had risen to 45 percent of the value of imports. Prior to the Arthur administration, rates were reduced, especially in 1857 by a Democratic Congress and President James Buchanan. In 1872, a Republican Congress, supported by President Grant, raised rates back up to an average of 39 percent.[26]

In the 1870s and into the 1880s, there was increasing debate over the economic consequences of a protective tariff. Most Republicans favored tariff rates high enough to protect American manufacturers and their workers from foreign competition, but a segment of the party argued that lower tariff rates would promote trade and would lower the cost of products made in this country. Most Democrats believed that lower tariff rates would lead to lower prices, but a wing of the party supported the protectionist stance.[27] The Republicans were better at controlling their minority than were the Democrats during these years. Only after Grover Cleveland brought in a Democratic administration in 1887 did that party unite seriously to support lower rates.

The Northeast and the upper Midwest, with most of the country's population and generating most of its wealth, supported the protective tariff, which most businesspeople and workers considered beneficial. Historically the South had supported low tariffs because of its agricultural exports—especially cotton, tobacco, and indigo. Southerners opposed protective tariffs that might provoke other countries to raise their tariffs on Southern exports. The South's influence in Congress, however, had not yet recovered from the Civil War. The sparsely populated Western states also favored low tariffs, but their political clout was no match for that of the Northeast and the upper Midwest.[28]

The economist David A. Wells (1828–1898), who favored sound money and *laissez-faire* policies, made the case for lower tariff rates. He argued that because America's domestic market could not absorb its industrial and agricultural output, the United States had to export, but exports would be hampered by high U.S. tariffs on imports. By 1876, he found himself more at home in the Democratic Party.

Agreeing with Wells in general was the Republican representative Horatio C. Burchard of Illinois, who stated that Americans had the advantage of "the superior intelligence of our labor, the inventive genius, and managing tact and skill of our people in applying and using labor-saving machinery and less expensive processes."[29]

Senator William Windom of Minnesota, Garfield's secretary of the treasury who did not get along with Arthur and had resigned, called for the government to expand the capabilities of America's internal waterways on which the "farmers of the interior of this continent are therefore wholly dependent...for a sale of their surplus grain."[30] He further believed that these public works would provide employment to relieve the impact of economic downturns[31]—a foretaste of New Deal thinking. Windom would again serve as secretary of the treasury under President Benjamin Harrison.

In his first annual message in 1881, Arthur called for modest reductions in tariff rates, asking Congress to authorize the president to appoint a commission of experts (from outside Congress) to propose changes in tariff policy. This was done, and the commissioners he selected, reflecting mostly the dominant Republican sentiment, favored what they saw as most conducive to thriving businesses. The chairman of the commission was John L. Hayes, secretary of the National Association of Wool Manufacturers and an advocate of tariff protection.[32]

In the summer of 1882, the commission held hearings at which most of those testifying opposed lower tariffs. Among the minority of free traders was the political economist William Graham Sumner of Yale, who advocated for an economic system free from government control and praised the benefits to the whole economy of the success of men such as J. P. Morgan, Andrew Carnegie, Cornelius Vanderbilt, and John D. Rockefeller.[33]

Arthur's advocacy of increasing trade with other countries was not controversial, but his position in favor of lower tariffs clashed with the majority sentiment in his party. The tariff commission recommended cuts in the rates of 20–25 percent, which Arthur supported. But Congress amended and amended until the final result, known as the "Mongrel Tariff," which passed in March 1883, brought in only slight reductions— a modest achievement, but the best that was possible at that time.

Arthur and others favoring lower tariff rates managed to moderate the protectionist laws but could not shake the prevailing political and economic case for high rates. A treaty to expand two-way trade with Mexico, submitted to the Senate in February 1883, was approved in March 1884 only after it was watered down out of fear that Mexican tobacco and sugar would bring unfair competition to American growers and that the president was trying to assume too much power. In his December 1884 message to Congress, Arthur again argued that lower tariff rates would increase foreign trade and improve the American economy. Once more, his clear thinking and courage won him plaudits, but not victory, in the political arena where the weakness of his base precluded success against protectionist interests. The controversy over tariff policy continues to this day, sharply dividing people philosophically, politically, and economically, as do the fights over other divisive issues that arose during the Arthur years.

CHAPTER 11

Reforming the Armed Forces

Rebuilding the navy was a front-burner issue for the Arthur administration. When the Civil War ended in 1865, the American navy was second in size only to Britain's. Thereafter the decline of the navy as well as the army was rapid, as Congress evinced only limited interest in funding a powerful force. National attention was focused on continental development and on coastal protection. No likely enemy confronted us, and overseas trade could rely on the relatively peaceful conditions enforced by the Royal Navy. The number of registered American ships did not recover quickly from the losses to Confederate raiders and from the increased cost of insurance caused by the war.[1] Before the Civil War, American ships carried two-thirds of the value of American exports. By 1870, that figure had dropped to one-third, and by 1880 to one-sixth. In 1882, Captain John Codman of Boston testified to a congressional committee:

> We have lost our prestige and experience: we are no longer a maritime nation, our shipowners have been wearied and disgusted; they have gone into other business, forced by their

government to abandon their old calling. Our ship masters, the pride of the ocean in the old packet days, are dead, and they have no successors.[2]

Shipping on inland waterways and along America's coasts flourished, but the costs of competing with foreign ships in overseas trade had yet to be corrected. More money could be earned in railroads and other segments of the economy. Between 1865 and 1881, Congress authorized only ten new ships for the navy.[3] Commander George Dewey, the future hero of Manila Bay, wrote of these years:

In the long period of inertia for our navy after the Civil War, while our country took no interest in its defenses and our ships did little cruising, officers saw relatively a great deal of shore duty.

We had no sea-going commerce to protect.... Our antiquated men-of-war had become the laughing stock of the nations.[4]

The Politics of Naval Reform

Andrew Johnson, a Democrat politically crippled by the Radical Republicans, could do little for the navy, and his immediate successors, Grant and Hayes, had little interest in reviving naval power. Going into the 1880s, the U.S. Navy ranked twelfth in the world, behind Turkey and Sweden.[5] In warship tonnage, it ranked fourth—behind Britain, France, and Russia—but much of that tonnage included obsolescent ships and coastal defense vessels incapable of protecting American overseas interests. At the same time, the American share of world manufacturing output was surpassed only by that of Britain.[6] Garfield gave some indication that he might bring an end to America's naval decline, but it is impossible to say what would have happened had he not been assassinated.

Garfield's secretary of the navy, William H. Hunt, came quickly to see that the decline had reached a critical stage and that the U.S. Navy was approaching absolute insignificance. He assembled an advisory board headed by Rear Admiral John Rogers and including Commander Robley Evans, who later commanded the battleship *Iowa* during the Spanish-American War and led the "Great White Fleet" on its epic round-the-world voyage of 1907–1909. Evans called for new ships to be steel, drawing the opposition of many hidebound higher-ranking naval officers. After heated debate, the motion carried.[7] Hunt now forged a consensus among naval officers and members of Congress that the country needed metal-hulled steam cruisers for coastal defense, showing the flag overseas during peacetime, and raiding enemy commerce if war became necessary. These ships additionally had to have sail capability since the United States at that time did not have overseas coaling stations. Of course, there would be disputes about how many new ships were needed and their size and capabilities. Hunt also proposed establishing the Office of Naval Intelligence, which was done shortly after he left office late in 1881.[8] Like all but one of Garfield's cabinet members, Hunt was replaced by Arthur.

The new secretary of the navy was William E. Chandler of New Hampshire, a Harvard Law School alumnus and a successful attorney. His love life was out of a romance novel. First, he fell in love with and married the daughter of Governor John Gilmore. After her death, he revived his relationship with Lucy Hale, a daughter of Senator John Hale, also of New Hampshire. She had been betrothed to John Wilkes Booth but had nothing to do with the plot to assassinate Lincoln. Now the old love between Chandler and Lucy was rekindled, and they married. Chandler served in the New Hampshire House of Representatives, becoming speaker. In 1865, President Andrew Johnson named him judge advocate general of the Navy Department and later appointed him assistant secretary of the treasury. When he returned to New Hampshire, Chandler edited and published a newspaper before heeding Arthur's call and returning to Washington. After his successful years in the Arthur administration, Chandler again returned to New Hampshire, where the legislature elected him to the United States Senate, and back he went to Washington.

Chester Arthur was convinced that for the United States to be prosperous, strong, and successful, the decline of its navy had to be reversed. Years of peace and no serious fears of foreign threats had bred complacency, an attitude that was increasingly dangerous as America's foreign trade grew. History is filled with examples of the danger of a weak navy for wealthy countries with extensive overseas trade. In his second annual address, delivered on December 4, 1882, Arthur reminded his countrymen of the urgency of rebuilding the navy, a task that required the revival of an American shipbuilding industry that had languished since the Civil War:

> This subject is one of the utmost importance to the national welfare. Methods of reviving American shipbuilding and of restoring the United States flag in the ocean carrying trade should receive the immediate attention of Congress. We have mechanical skill and abundant material for the manufacture of modern iron steamships in fair competition with our commercial rivals. Our disadvantage in building ships is the greater cost of labor, and in sailing them, higher taxes, and greater interest on capital, while the ocean highways are already monopolized by our formidable competitors. These obstacles should in some way be overcome, and for our rapid communication with foreign lands we should not continue to depend wholly upon vessels built in the yards of other countries and sailing under foreign flags. With no United States steamers on the principal ocean lines or in any foreign ports, our facilities for extending our commerce are greatly restricted, while the nations which build and sail the ships and carry the mails and passengers obtain thereby conspicuous advantages in increasing their trade.[9]

He further called for the transfer of the lighthouse service and coast survey, as well as the operation of revenue service ships capable of operating offshore, from the Treasury Department to the navy.[10] Arthur's foresight and determination should be more greatly appreciated.

In his last annual message to Congress, in 1884, Arthur again argued for a powerful navy, warning that "the long peace that has lulled us into a sense of fancied security may at any time be disturbed."[11]

American relations with the United Kingdom were good; the two countries shared key values and did not pose a threat to each other's interests. The British had the most powerful navy in the world, the largest empire (about a quarter of the world's population and land mass), and the strongest economy. British policy was to develop a navy equal to the next two fleets combined. Furthermore, the British were the greatest manufacturing power in the world, had the largest merchant marine, and led the world in banking.[12] France was reviving but was focused on Europe and on parts of the world of less importance to the United States. In addition, friendship between the United States and France dated back to our alliance with them during our war for independence.

Beyond these two powers, the prospects for conflict were real. Germany and Japan, like the United States, were expanding their influence in the Pacific. Russia, too, was aggressive and expansionist but less interested in the Pacific than in Europe, the Middle East, and the Far East.

But the likeliest source of conflict in the near future was Spain. In decline since the late sixteenth century but still controlling an extensive empire, it resented both the rise of the United States as a power in the Americas and the independence movement that had cost it most of its colonies there. Spain still ruled Cuba and Puerto Rico and was willing to fight the United States to keep them. American opinion opposed Spanish repression and favored either the United States' accession of Cuba and Puerto Rico or their independence. To have any influence, America needed a far better navy. The Arthur administration started the navy on the way back.

Building New Ships

When he took office, Arthur supported Chandler's moves to clean up the mess that his predecessor, Hunt, had identified. Navy yard corruption was widespread, as happens all too often when the spending of taxpayer money is not carefully supervised. Crews of ships contained many foreign nationals, and their officers all too often were old men who had risen because of seniority.[13] By no means was reform immediate, but a new era had begun.

Part of Chandler's effort to root out corruption and bring in efficiency was his call for Congress to spend less on repairing older ships. Such repairs were a handy way for congressmen to reward friends with government contracts and jobs, however, and the proposal attracted strong opposition. But the navy was repairing ships that were too old for use against any modern enemy. A midshipman on the *Richmond* in 1883 called his vessel a "poor excuse for a tub, unarmored, with pop-guns for a battery and a crew composed of the refuse of all nations, three-quarters of whom cannot speak intelligible English."[14]

Officers of higher rank often were aged, but there was a strong sense of professionalism among naval officers. Nevertheless, there was an overabundance of them. The Naval Academy at Annapolis graduated well-trained officers, but there were too many of them for the ships and shore assignments available.

Arthur and Chandler's determination to modernize the navy received a major boost from a measure introduced by Representative George Robeson of New Jersey, who had served as secretary of the navy under Grant. It funded two cruisers and five coastal defense monitors and prohibited spending more than thirty percent of a ship's replacement cost on repairs. All too often, national security considerations took a backseat as government contracts to repair old ships were considered primarily as sources of revenue for contractors and jobs for shipyard workers. The measure passed in August 1882, and the Survey and Inspection Board of the navy promptly condemned forty-four ships—about a third of those in service.[15]

In the 1882 election, the Republicans retained the Senate but lost control of the House. The following March, the lame-duck Republican majority passed a bill authorizing three protected cruisers, the 4,500-ton *Chicago*, the 3,189-ton *Atlanta* and *Boston*, and the 1,500-ton dispatch boat *Dolphin*. The *Chicago*, 342 feet long, carried four eight-inch guns, eight six-inch guns, and two five-inch guns. The *Atlanta* and the *Boston* were 283 feet in length and armed with two eight-inch guns and six six-inch guns.

Chandler appointed Rear Admiral Robert W. Shufeldt (1822–1895), president of the second Naval Advisory Board, which was to superintend the construction of these ships. The administration hoped to get one of them in commission before the end of Arthur's term, but they missed the target. The three were launched in 1884 and commissioned in 1885 when Cleveland was president. They formed the Squadron of Evolution, popularly known as the "White Squadron" because of their white hulls. The navy refused to accept the *Dolphin* because of too many construction defects, though it eventually entered service and performed well, sailing around the world in 1888–1889 with only one minor engine correction needed. The three cruisers, too, had problems, and their completion was taken over by the navy. Like the *Dolphin*, they proved themselves sound ships.[16]

The contract for building the four ships had been awarded to John Roach, a major contributor to Chandler and other Republicans, who was the low bidder. A combination of corruption and his inability to handle the project drove him into bankruptcy and hurt the Republicans in the 1884 election. There is no clear evidence of any culpability on Arthur's part. It further appears that Chandler was not guilty of wrongdoing beyond awarding the contracts to someone who had helped Republicans in the past but could not deliver.[17] This scandal was one of the factors propelling Grover Cleveland to victory over James G. Blaine in the presidential election of 1884.

Still, there is no question that the Arthur administration halted the decline of the U.S. Navy. The three cruisers indicated America's intent to become a naval power that could protect its citizens and its interests worldwide.

Submarines

Less impressive was the limited interest of the navy in submarines during the Arthur years. This soon would change as the development of undersea warfare sped up and the opportunities and dangers became more evident. The human drive to do what never before has been done, to go where no one has gone, eventually inspired the development of vessels that could submerge and attack enemy ships from below. As far back as the late sixteenth century, the Englishman William Bourne was theorizing how a vessel might submerge and resurface. In 1623, the Dutchman Cornelis Drebbel built what most likely was the first successful submarine. The American David Bushnell designed and constructed the first submarine to attack a warship. It launched an unsuccessful attack in 1775 on one of the British ships blockading New York during the American Revolution. During the Civil War, the first sinking of an enemy warship was scored by the Confederate *Hunley*, later lost in action with all hands.[18]

By the time of Arthur's presidency, progress was increasing. John Philip Holland, born in Ireland, immigrated to the United States in 1873. In 1878, he built a fourteen-foot one-man submarine funded by the Irish Republican Brotherhood and the Fenians, who wanted the means to challenge the Royal Navy in the fight for Irish independence. In 1881, Holland launched a larger vessel, this one thirty-one feet long with a crew of three—an operator, an engineer, and a gunner who controlled a nine-inch air-propelled gun. Over the next two years, tests were successful as the boat reached depths of sixty feet and remained submerged for as long as an hour. In 1883, a naval officer, Lieutenant William K. Kimball, who read of Holland's work, tried unsuccessfully to get the Navy Department to hire him.[19] Further progress by the U.S. Navy in submarine development had to wait until the mid-1890s during Grover Cleveland's second term.

The Greely Expedition

Helping to build public support for the navy was the rescue of survivors of the Greely expedition. Twenty-five men under Lieutenant Adolphus Greely of the U.S. Army Signal Corps sailed on the *Proteus* in the summer of 1881 to northwest Greenland and then west to Lady Franklin Bay in the Canadian arctic, where they disembarked to conduct scientific observations. Carrying supplies for three years, they were to be picked up by the *Proteus* after two years. If that were not possible, the men were to head south on their own, subsisting on supplies dropped at several locations along their route. In the summer of 1883, the *Proteus* reached Cape Sabine, two hundred miles south of Greely's base, but did not land supplies before being sunk by the ice.[20] The expedition now headed south along the eastern coast of Ellesmere Island, finding some supply caches left by other expeditions, but too little to sustain them.

The plight of the Greely expedition by then was world news. Secretary of the Navy Chandler organized a rescue effort led by Commander Winfield Scott Schley, who later would play a prominent and controversial role in the victory over the Spanish at Santiago in 1898. The state of the American navy was exposed by the necessity of purchasing two whalers and of Britain's contribution of a steamer. The relief flotilla sailed on May 1, 1884, and on June 22 reached Greely and the six other survivors.[21] Their return to New York was triumphal. Reports that the survivors had resorted to cannibalism, denied by Greely although probably true, did not dim their luster. Greely went on to a distinguished career. In 1886, Grover Cleveland promoted him from captain to brigadier general, just as Theodore Roosevelt would do a few years later with John Pershing—still an extraordinarily rare jump in rank. He served as the chief signal officer in the army and retired in 1908 as a major general. On March 21, 1935, not long before his death, he was awarded the Congressional Medal of Honor for "lifetime achievement." He and Charles Lindbergh are the only persons to receive this honor who did not earn it in combat.[22]

The crisis of the Greely party and the inability of the navy to mount a rescue operation supported the Arthur administration's case that the revival of the navy was a national necessity. Events and effective leadership were slowly changing public attitudes.

The Naval War College and a New Sea Power

Encouragement came near the end of Arthur's term when Chandler approved the plan submitted by Commodore Stephen B. Luce (1827–1917) to establish the Naval War College. In October 1884, Luce was appointed the first president of the institution, located in Newport, Rhode Island. Having begun his naval service in 1841 as a midshipman, Luce was a member of the first class when the U.S. Naval Academy opened at Annapolis in 1845, graduating in 1849. Between assignments at sea during the Civil War, he commanded the Naval Academy training ship. When Arthur became president in 1881, Luce, now a commodore, commanded the Naval Training Squadron.[23]

Back in 1877, Luce had written to Secretary of the Navy Michael W. Thompson calling for "the establishment of a school wherein our junior officers shall be carried through a post graduate course consisting of the higher branches of their profession."[24] He argued that naval officers were not being taught naval strategy and history at an advanced enough level. Many senior officers, men who had risen by seniority and now were rather hidebound and ossified, had opposed the school. On the faculty was captain, later admiral, Alfred Thayer Mahan (1840–1914), already a well-known naval thinker who within a few years would be recognized as the foremost naval historian and theoretician in the world. In 1883, his rather pedantic Civil War study, *The Gulf and Inland Waters,* caught the attention of Luce, who selected him for the new school. His 1887 lectures here would be published in 1890 as *The Influence of Sea Power upon History: 1660–1783*. It became the most influential geopolitical study in the world, lauded, for example, by Theodore Roosevelt and Kaiser Wilhelm II. The book was required reading for naval and military leaders from the Americas through Europe to Asia. Also on the staff of the war college was Lieutenant Tasker Bliss (1853–1930), a West Point graduate and a scholar who would rise to be chief of staff in World War I.

In *The Influence of Sea Power upon History: 1660–1783*, Mahan argued that great navies were the decisive factor in the growth of the British, French, Dutch, and Spanish empires. When he wrote, the British Empire was the greatest in the world primarily because the Royal Navy defended the realm against foreign invasion, protected British trade, and facilitated the spread of British influence throughout the world.

The United States enjoyed the same advantages that had made Britain a world power. First, its geographical location spared it from major enemies on its borders. Second, it had an extensive coastline with many excellent harbors. Third, many Americans loved the oceans and were experienced sailors. Fourth, Americans were by nature a bold, hardworking people with a knack for trade. And fifth, freedom provided opportunity and fostered achievement. Mahan did recognize the damage to America's once-great merchant fleet by Confederate raiders during the Civil War and crippling insurance rates that harmed American ships. He was adamant that America's navy and merchant marine had to be rebuilt for the United States to become a true world power.[25]

Future Admirals

In addition to Schley and Mahan, two other future admirals, George Dewey (1837–1917) and William Sampson (1840–1902), played important roles in Arthur's rebuilding of the navy. Like Schley and Mahan, they were graduates of the Naval Academy, veterans of the Civil War, and all survived as professional sailors during the postwar years of neglect of the armed forces. In 1884, Dewey was promoted to captain and given command of the previously-mentioned *Dolphin*. During Arthur's presidency, Commander Sampson was assistant to the superintendent of the naval observatory, represented the United States at the international conference that settled the Greenwich prime meridian, and was assigned to Newport, Rhode Island, as commander of the torpedo station and inspector of ordinance.[26] In the Spanish-American War, Dewey would command the American naval forces in the victory at Manila Bay. Sampson commanded in the victory at Santiago with Schley as his second in command.

An excellent case can be made that Arthur's most important accomplishment as president was reversing America's naval decline and putting the country on the path to world power. By 1900, the United States had surged into first place in manufacturing and had risen impressively among the navies of the world. By the early twentieth century, only the British and German fleets were larger. During World War I, the United States moved ahead of the Germans, and during World War II, the U.S. Navy became the most powerful in the world— a position it still holds.[27] Arthur deserves more recognition for this renewal than he has received.

Building up the Army

The army attracted less attention from Arthur than did the navy, there being no realistic threats of land invasion. The Royal Navy was the most powerful fleet in the world, and our relations with Britain were good. The Arthur administration did, though, support some reforms which were facilitated by the friendship and mutual respect between Arthur and Secretary of War Robert Todd Lincoln, who served through both the Garfield and Arthur administrations. For example, steps were taken to modernize state militias with better equipment and training, assigning regular army officers to work with them.[28]

The improvements of the Arthur years were real, but in the 1880s there was not a substantial political base of support for any major deployment of the army overseas. The quality of the regular army was good, but it was small, and state militias, in general, were not trained and equipped to supplement the regulars in a serious conflict. In 1898, as the country prepared for war with Spain, Nelson Miles, the commanding general of the army, warned that most of the states "have made no provision for their...militia, and not one is fully equipped for field service."[29]

Robert Todd Lincoln was a constructive change from his predecessors in the office of the previous two decades. Since the end of the Civil War, the secretaries of war and of the navy had been strictly political appointees—men with limited knowledge of the armed services. Two secretaries of the navy, Hunt and Chandler, were determined to reverse the decay in that service even if they had not worn the uniform. Lincoln shared their determination for improvement and did have some experience on active duty. When the Civil War began, he was near the end of his first year at Harvard. One of his three brothers had died in 1850, and a second would die in 1862, both of natural causes. His mother was terrified at the prospect of losing another, a sentiment his father supported. Finally, after Robert graduated from college and spent a semester at Harvard Law School, both parents finally relented, and he joined the army on February 11, 1865. A captain and assistant adjutant general of volunteers, he served on General Grant's staff.[30]

On May 7, 1881, a few weeks before Garfield was shot, William Tecumseh Sherman, general in chief of the army, issued an order establishing the School of Application for Infantry and Cavalry at Fort Leavenworth, Kansas.[31] The army already had advanced training centers for engineers and artillery. This step by Sherman enhanced the country's preparedness to face a serious adversary. The total numbers in the service remained small, but now there would be a nucleus of prepared leaders whenever the need arose. This was especially important as the Civil War faded into history and the many veterans of that conflict aged. For the present, that generation still led. The army had one full general, Sherman, one lieutenant general, Philip Sheridan, and three major generals—Irvin McDowell, Winfield Scott Hancock, and John Schofield. All had held field command positions in the Civil War, compiling records ranging from respectable to outstanding.

These improvements were constructive, although when the United States went to war with Spain, shortcomings in equipment and in the training of national guard units still had to be overcome. All too often, Americans have not planned for the possibility of armed conflict with foreign enemies. In 1898, the United States went to war with a navy growing in size and skill since the Arthur years and with an army that had improved in organization, training, and leadership during that same period. But the army was not ready for the extraordinarily rapid increase in size necessitated by the war with Spain, a war the United States entered with far smaller numbers than its opponent.[32]

Qualitatively the regular army was impressive, especially the West Point–educated officer corps. Of these regulars, Richard Harding Davis wrote, "The manner in which each man handled his horse or musket, and especially himself, made you proud that they were American soldiers, and desperately sorry that there were so few of them."[33]

During Arthur's presidency, the United States maintained a peacetime army. Large numbers were not involved in the Apache campaign. About half the officers holding rank from major through brigadier general held staff positions.[34] This reflects both the bureaucratic sclerosis which can afflict any army at times of peace and the legitimate maintenance of a nucleus that can organize a rapid expansion in times of war. The caliber of the rank and file was less impressive, a large percentage of them being men who could not find good civilian jobs—especially recent immigrants from Europe.

Robert Lincoln earned respect for introducing more efficiency and energy into the War Department. General Richard C. Drum, the adjutant general of the army, called Lincoln "the best secretary of war we have had since Jefferson Davis."[35] Since Davis had served from 1853 to 1857, this was meaningful praise. The expansion of the army, however, would lag well behind that of the navy. It temporarily surged during the 1898 war with Spain, declined again until World War I, and shrank again until World War II, following which the need for constant readiness became a reality.

CHAPTER 12

Central American Canal

While Arthur was strengthening the navy, he recognized that a canal through Central America controlled by the United States would be an enormous strategic and economic advantage. Interest in a canal linking the Atlantic and the Pacific dated back to 1513, when Vasco Núñez de Balboa led his expedition from the Caribbean shore of Panama to the Pacific. He saw the obvious strategic and trade advantages of a canal across the isthmus.

In the 1840s, the expansion of the United States to the Pacific after the Mexican War and the discovery of gold in California fanned American interest in the project. Panama was then part of New Granada, which in a few years would change its name to the United States of Colombia. In 1848, the American ambassador, Benjamin A. Bidlack, negotiated a treaty with New Granada stipulating, "The right of way or transit across the Isthmus of Panama, upon any modes of communication that now exist, or that may be...constructed, shall be open and free to the Government and citizens of the United States."[1] In return, the United States agreed that the territory would remain part of New Granada and pledged to defend the neutrality of the isthmus and free transit across it.[2]

In 1849, the American-owned Panama Railroad Company secured a ninety-nine-year concession to build and operate a railroad from Aspinwall (later Colón) on the Caribbean to Panama City on the Pacific. The line, forty-eight miles long, began service in 1855.³ The travel and trade advantages were obvious, and business was brisk.

In 1850, the administration of Zachary Taylor negotiated the Clayton-Bulwer Treaty with Britain stipulating that the two countries would share equally in a Central American canal, that neither would fortify it, and that both would refrain from seeking to spread their power in the region. These terms favored the British since they already held territory in the Caribbean area—including British Honduras, now Belize. The treaty was not popular in the United States, many considering it too favorable to British interests. At any rate, no action was taken.

Distant from most of Colombia's population and economic activity, the Panamanians developed a sense of separateness and a desire for independence strengthened by resentment over seeing revenue generated by isthmus transit leaving Panama. This sentiment led to a number of revolts during the second half of the nineteenth century, but the Panamanians failed to secure independence, and the United States stopped short of intervention on their behalf.

President Grant, in his first message to Congress, called for a canal across Central America and for the United States to build it. "To Europeans the benefits of the proposed canal are great," he said, "To Americans they are invaluable."⁴ The project languished, though, beset by difficulties in securing financing and overcoming the rugged terrain of Panama. Congressional support for the canal was weakened by railroad interests, which disliked the competition it would bring.

Grant's successor, Rutherford Hayes, also supported building a canal, emphasizing too that the United States must control it. In March 1880, just as French interests were securing an agreement with Panama for the canal, he told Congress:

> The United States cannot consent to the surrender of this control to any European power or any combination of

European powers. The capital invested by corporations or citizens of other countries in such an enterprise must in a great degree look for protection to one or more of the great powers of the world. No European power can intervene for such protection without adopting measures on this continent which the United States would deem wholly inadmissible.[5]

The United States had the desire to limit European power in the Americas but lacked the means—a strong navy. As it turned out, rivalries between the major powers in other parts of the world and America's friendship with Britain, the strongest of all, limited the danger of European incursions in the Western Hemisphere until the United States had built a navy commensurate with its economy.

Meanwhile, others moved to make the dream of a canal a reality. The Frenchman Ferdinand de Lesseps, the builder of the Suez Canal, became intrigued by the prospect of linking the Atlantic and the Pacific. In 1882 work began, but the project broke down in 1889 with ten percent of the canal completed, defeated by a number of factors. For one thing, money and time were wasted trying to build a sea-level canal before it became clear that a system of locks was necessary. Financial corruption drained away more funds. A final blow was the ravages of tropical diseases such as yellow fever.

As the de Lesseps Panama Canal enterprise was encountering increasing difficulties, the Arthur administration remained determined to build a canal. The efforts of Secretary of State Frelinghuysen at last paid dividends on December 1, 1884, when a treaty was signed with Nicaragua for a canal across its territory. Although the distance to be covered was wider in Nicaragua than in Panama, much of the distance was taken up by Lake Nicaragua, so the amount of excavation would be comparable.[6] At this point, Arthur was a lame duck, having lost the Republican nomination to James G. Blaine, who in turn lost to Grover Cleveland in November. When Arthur submitted the treaty to the Senate on December 10, he argued that there were important economic and military reasons for completing a canal:

> Forming one nation in interests and aims, the East and the
> West are more widely disjoined for all purposes of direct and
> economical intercourse by water and of national defense
> against maritime aggression than are most of the colonies of
> other powers from their mother country.[7]

He went on to affirm, "The political effect of the canal will be to
knit closer the States now depending upon railway corporations for all
commercial and personal intercourse...."[8]

Under the treaty, the United States would pay to build the canal,
which would be owned jointly by the two countries and administered by
a six-man board—three Americans and three Nicaraguans. The United
States would receive two-thirds of the profits, Nicaragua one-third. The
canal zone, two and a half miles wide, would be jointly owned, with
Americans in control militarily. This last provision was to keep an
aggressive foreign country from seizing the canal from a militarily weak
Nicaragua and to ensure its continued operation in spite of the frequent
military coups in the region.

Arthur made it clear that the United States did not seek Nicaraguan
territory and would work with Nicaragua as a partner.[9] Nevertheless,
the wealth and size of the United States would make it the stronger partner, even though nothing to that effect was in the treaty. The Senate
approved the treaty by a vote of thirty-two to twenty-three, short of the
two-thirds margin needed for ratification. The chairman of the Foreign
Relations Committee, John F. Miller of California, supported the administration's foreign policy. The second-ranking member, John Sherman of
Ohio, had supported Blaine but also favored U.S. expansion. Across the
aisle, the treaty was backed by John T. Morgan of Alabama and George
H. Pendleton of Ohio. Leading the Democratic opposition in the Senate
was Thomas F. Bayard of Delaware, soon to be secretary of state under
Cleveland.

The prospects for passage were complicated by disagreement over
where the canal should be built and whether it should be paid for by the

government or by private investors. Above all was the problem that Arthur was a lame duck.[10]

The new president, Grover Cleveland, withdrew the treaty, stating that a canal should be "a trust for mankind, to be removed from the chance of domination by any single power."[11] Some two decades later, American policy would change dramatically under Theodore Roosevelt, who was keen on making the United States a world power.

CHAPTER 13

Foreign Policy

S ecretary of State James G. Blaine left the cabinet in December 1881 by agreement between himself and Arthur. Probably still unaware of his affliction with Bright's disease, Arthur was looking ahead to running for a term of his own in 1884 and was well aware of Blaine's ambitions for the same office—ambitions that had been thwarted in 1876 and in 1880. Both men understood political reality. It would be impossibly awkward for Blaine to serve a president he intended to defeat unless that president were a fool or a weakling, and Arthur was neither.

A Congress of the Americas

Blaine had proposed a congress of the countries of the Americas, an idea Arthur initially supported. As he settled into the presidency, however, he changed his mind. The new secretary of state, Frederick T. Frelinghuysen, also opposed the congress. Though Blaine favored leadership by the United States in the Western Hemisphere, he envisioned America "as a single member among many coordinate and coequal states" in the congress,[1] apparently unaware of any contradiction in these positions. He assumed that the other countries would voluntarily follow U.S. leadership. For the rest of Arthur's term, Blaine was back in private life preparing for the 1884 Republican National Convention. Arthur had made it clear that he was president, that the administration was his.

Foreign policy was not a subject of major interest for most Americans during Arthur's presidency. But the United States, which would astound the world with its victory over Spain in 1898, was showing signs of becoming more than just a continental power, thanks in part to Arthur's naval reforms.

Ireland

Widespread sympathy in Britain for the Confederacy had strained Anglo-American relations during the Civil War, but relations had improved after the war. There were still some stresses, however, one of the most contentious being the strong anti-British sentiment of immigrants from Ireland. Most of them integrated into American society, but a few, after becoming American citizens, returned to Ireland and involved themselves in politics, determined to secure Irish independence from Britain. Some moved beyond politics, taking up arms against what they considered to be an oppressive occupier. From the British perspective, this was rebellion against lawful government. This involvement of American citizens introduced tensions between the United States and the United Kingdom. The Arthur administration appreciated the degree of anti-British feeling among Irish-Americans and the political hazards it posed.

Subjected to intense pressure from both sides, the administration settled on a policy intended to be both fair and neutral. Naturalized Americans who returned to Ireland to live, to become involved in politics, and, in some cases, to hold office, were subject to the law there. The administration did insist on prompt and fair legal procedures for those charged with offenses.[2]

Mexico

Mexico, its government unable to ensure stability and protect freedom, continued to be a lure for expansionist-minded Americans and a headache for those who wanted normal, peaceful relations with the United States' southern neighbor. Linguistic and cultural differences complicated relations with the United States, but more troubling was the Mexican fluctuation between dictatorship and chaos.

Mexico, though, attracted the interest not only of the principled Americans who hoped to see order, justice, and freedom thrive there but also that of the avaricious. Some Americans saw the opportunity to make money by dealing with Mexican dictators such as Porfirio Díaz, who dominated the country from 1876 until 1911. He established order and stability and improved relations with the United States by making payments on American claims and by controlling cross-border raids by Mexican bandits. The economy grew under his rule, with improvements in transportation, industrialization, and trade, as well as in oil wells and mines. Foreign investment, especially from Britain, the United States, and France, was responsible for most of this. The cost, however, was high. There was little freedom, and the lower classes had few opportunities to rise.

The trade treaty with Mexico that was signed during Arthur's last year in office did some good. It was probably the best Arthur could have done with his limited political clout late in his administration.[3]

Africa

European powers were continuing to expand their empires into Africa, a process that eventually left only two independent countries on the continent—Liberia, sponsored by Americans as a home for freed slaves, and the ancient Christian monarchy of Ethiopia. The Congo had not come under the sway of the major powers, which were occupied with more strategically important and economically valuable lands. When Belgium moved in, these other powers acquiesced, happy to avoid the clash that would be likely if one of them had expanded its empire into central Africa. That clash might be postponed, but it would not be prevented. In 1878, King Leopold II hired the Welshman Henry Morton Stanley, who had previously explored the region, to set up outposts on the Congo River.

For Americans, the prospects here were more alluring than those in territories controlled by one of the major powers—Britain, France, and Germany. In his 1883 annual message, Arthur called for American involvement in opening the Congo economically without getting drawn into political complications, although he quite likely understood the difficulty of trying to keep them separate. Supporting this position, albeit for a narrower set of reasons, was Senator John T. Morgan, a Democrat from Alabama. He saw the Congo as a market for Southern textile mills and as a place to send freed slaves.[4] For these reasons, Morgan backed the repressive colonial rule of Leopold, for whom the Congo was a vast personal estate rather than a colony of Belgium. Also calling for the United States to adopt a more assertive stance in the world beyond its shores was John Kasson, the American minister to Austria-Hungary. He believed there was a worldwide struggle for export markets and that the United States had no alternative to aggressively pursuing them.[5]

In *The Scramble for Africa: 1876–1912*, Thomas Pakenham argued that Arthur and the Americans were hoodwinked by Leopold into believing that slavery would be suppressed and that the constitution of the Congo would be based on America's.[6] While it certainly was true that the United States opposed slavery and supported freedom, its policy was based on the opportunities for expanding its exports and gaining better access to raw materials. Arthur, his administration, and Congress may not have seen through Leopold's machinations or foreseen that a repressive regime would be imposed on the Congo, but Americans were not simple innocents being manipulated.

In November 1884, German chancellor Otto von Bismarck convened a conference in Berlin to avoid clashes between European powers over the Congo. His paramount interest was strengthening Germany's primacy in Europe, which entailed not antagonizing the British and pushing them into an anti-German alliance. Furthermore, the French domination of Europe from the seventeenth century through the Napoleonic era fueled his determination to keep France isolated. Bismarck further considered it essential to keep Russia neutral, if not friendly, preventing a Franco-Russian alliance that could force Germany into a two-front war.

Arthur appointed Kasson, the American representative, to the Berlin Conference. The French and the Portuguese countered Leopold with their own claims on the Congo, but the United States supported Leopold, who left the conference with the Congo still his. This was satisfactory to Germany, which did not want France to occupy it or Portugal, which was allied to Britain; Belgium was neutral. For the United States, Belgian control of the Congo was preferable to control by one of the major European powers. Kasson wanted an American base in the Congo, a position only partially supported by Secretary of State Frelinghuysen, who did order the U.S. Navy to check out locations for "a commercial resort."[7]

Arthur's support for the conclusions of the Berlin Conference reflected an ambitious view of America's role in the world that would eventually prevail under the administrations of McKinley and Theodore Roosevelt. But for now, it was a minority view, and Arthur was a lame duck president. James G. Blaine, who had replaced him as the Republican standard-bearer in 1884 and then lost to Grover Cleveland, opposed Senate ratification of the conference's General Act, fuming acerbically, "How can we maintain the Monroe Doctrine when we take part in conferences on the internal affairs of other continents? We shall either be told some day to mind our own business or else be forced to admit governments to participation in the questions affecting America."[8] When Cleveland took office, he withdrew the treaty from consideration, and extensive American involvement in matters beyond its shores came to an end until 1898.

The Pacific

With the purchase of Alaska from Russia in 1867, the United States had expanded beyond its continental borders. Other than this extraordinary acquisition, its overseas possessions were limited to several small islands and atolls in the Pacific that were occupied under the Guano Islands Act of 1856, which authorized the government to plant the flag on these unoccupied islands from which the United States could acquire guano, a fertilizer. Baker Island, Howland Island, Jarvis Island, Johnston Atoll, Midway Atoll, Palmyra Atoll, and Kingman Reef supported American commercial ships, and later aircraft. These islands were strategically important in World War II, but they remain uninhabited except for personnel temporarily stationed for scientific studies.

During the two decades prior to 1898, there was little support in Congress or among the public for the overseas expansion of American power even as European countries, soon joined by Japan, were extending their domains. There was, though, a growing recognition by more American leaders that the alternative to American intervention was not peaceful freedom for these people, but was their falling under the sway of someone else. Two strategic Pacific territories that attracted U.S. attention were Hawaii and Samoa. Both were independent monarchies when Arthur was president, but those days were coming to an end as American interest and influence grew.

Hawaii offered a base for projecting power throughout the eastern and central Pacific. Polynesian explorers reached and occupied the islands about two thousand years ago, but they were unknown to Europeans until Captain James Cook of Britain came upon them in January 1778. The Hawaiians were devastated by European diseases such as measles and smallpox, to which they had no resistance, and the native population fell from an estimated 300,000 when the Europeans arrived to 108,000 in 1836 and 73,000 thousand in 1853. Outsiders from the United States, Japan, China, and Europe then moved in, and the native Hawaiians became a minority.

King Kamehameha I united the islands by military conquest, a task completed by 1810. He died in 1819 and was succeeded by his son

Kamehameha II, who ended the establishment of the old Hawaiian religion, gave his subjects freedom of religion, and became a Christian. After his death in 1824, his brother succeeded him as Kamehameha III. He made Christianity the official faith of the realm and made Hawaii a constitutional monarchy. The United States formally recognized the government in 1842, and Britain and France followed suit. Struggling to maintain its independence over the next several decades, Hawaii took advantage of the rivalries between the major powers. America, less distracted by expansion into other parts of the world, overtook Britain, France, Germany, and Japan in influence in Hawaii. That influence continued to expand through American Christian missionaries, American business activities, and immigrants moving there from the United States. The *New York Times* declared in an editorial on July 13, 1881:

> Although our government cannot afford to promote any policy of annexation, other Governments of the world should be notified that any attempt on their part to acquire the Sandwich Islands [Hawaii], by purchase or otherwise, would be regarded by the United States as an unfriendly act.[9]

David Kalakaua ascended the throne in 1874. During his reign, the longstanding American interest in establishing a naval base at Pearl Harbor, near Honolulu, the Hawaiian capital, became a reality. In 1840, Commodore Charles Wilkes had stated that if deepened, Pearl Harbor would be "the best and most capacious harbor in the Pacific."[10] The Arthur administration accepted Hawaiian independence but was determined to keep any other country from bringing Hawaii into its sphere of influence, let alone annexing it. In November 1881, Secretary of State Blaine set forth that position:

> The United States regards the Hawaiian group as essentially a part of the American system of states, and the key to the North Pacific trade, and...while favorably inclined toward

the continuance of native rule on a basis of political independence and commercial assimilation with the United States,
we could not regard the intrusion of any non-American interest in Hawaii as consistent with our relations thereto.[11]

After years of pondering and talking, a treaty was signed and ratified
in 1887, giving the United States the right to build the Pearl Harbor base
in return for the access of Hawaiian agricultural exports to U.S. markets.
A small country with weak armed forces and which occupied a strategic
location had limited options.

In 1891, Liliuokalani became queen upon the death of her brother
David Kalakaua. She sought to increase her powers by doing away with
the 1887 constitution, which permitted foreign citizens to vote if they
met residency requirements. In early 1893, she attempted to impose a
new constitution that had been rejected by the legislature. Opposed by
her cabinet as well, she found herself with little support from the people
of the islands, most of whom recognized that Hawaii had little hope for
continued independence. One of the major powers would occupy this
strategic location, and the United States was the best of the options.

Among the Americans who became more and more influential in
Hawaii, Sanford Dole, the son of American missionaries and born in the
islands, was the most important. Educated in the United States, he
returned to Hawaii as a lawyer, later serving in the legislature and as a
justice on the Supreme Court of Hawaii. He was elected president when
Hawaii was established as a republic. The government petitioned for
admission to the United States. In 1898, the petition was accepted and
Hawaii became an American territory.

Samoa, also an independent monarchy occupying a strategic position
in the Pacific, was discovered by Europeans in the early 1700s. Here too,
Christian missionary efforts were successful. Concerned that growing
British and German influence in the Pacific would curtail American trade
and influence there, the Grant administration moved to ensure the United
States' position. In 1872, Commander R. N. Meade arrived at Pago Pago,

the Samoan capital, as the representative of the U.S. government. He negotiated a treaty giving his country exclusive rights to establish a naval base there in return for protecting the independence of Samoa. The treaty, though, was rejected by the Senate, which was leery of the entanglement in conflicts that might follow from a guarantee of Samoan freedom. Complicating the prospects for success was a personal feud between Grant and Charles Sumner, the chairman of the Senate Foreign Relations Committee.[12]

During the next few years, American influence in Samoa increased, as did concerns that U.S. interests would be harmed were another country to seize control. In 1878, the Senate approved a treaty with Samoa giving the United States the right to use Pago Pago as a fueling station for both naval and commercial vessels. In return, the United Sates would mediate disputes between Samoa and other countries.[13]

In July 1881, the American consul, Thomas M. Dawson, brought together rival Samoan leaders on board the USS *Lackawanna*, one of the ships assigned to protect U.S. interests. Joining the conference were foreign consuls assigned to Samoa. The intent was to end the tension and strife and to bring about peaceful unity. One of the chiefs, Malietoa Laupepa, emerged as the choice to step in as king. Dawson further proposed to Secretary of State Blaine that the United States proclaim a protectorate over the islands, assuring him that it would be welcomed by the Samoans. Blaine, however, rejected taking that step. Conditions remained relatively stable as the consuls of the United States, the United Kingdom, and Germany cooperated enough to prevent disintegration and to preserve, at least outwardly, Samoan independence. Later in 1881, John Lundon, an ambitious New Zealander seeking to enhance both his own position and the British Empire, proposed that Samoa be annexed. This the British government refused to do, being more concerned about German expansion and, therefore, not wanting to antagonize the United States.[14]

In 1899, Samoa was divided between the United States and Germany. During World War I, prior to the American entry, New Zealand occupied

German Samoa. In 1962, that territory became independent. American Samoa voted to stay American, electing its governor and legislature.

As in its relations with Hawaii, the Arthur administration did nothing attention-grabbing, simply pursuing the ability to project American power, military and economic, in pursuit of U.S. interests in lands beyond our shores. Expressing this view, Representative Fernando Wood of New York proclaimed, "The Pacific Ocean is an American ocean, destined to hold a far higher place in the future of the world than the Atlantic. It is the future great highway between ourselves and the hundreds of millions of Asiatics who look to us for commerce, civilization, and Christianity."[15]

Note again the evident strength of Christianity and the confidence in expressing adherence to it. There was less fear then that such a statement would suggest the "establishment of religion" prohibited by the First Amendment.

Asia

While Britain, France, Japan, and Russia pursued territorial expansion at the cost of the declining Chinese empire, the United States expanded its influence through diplomacy and trade. The British had seized Hong Kong Island in 1842 and would expand their territory in 1860 and in 1898. France solidified its control of Indochina in the early and mid-1880s, pushing the Chinese back north. Japan was spreading its tentacles; within a few years, it would seize Taiwan and Korea and drive Russia out of Manchuria. But in the last decades of the nineteenth century, Russia still was moving into what had been Chinese territory. The United States alone among the major powers wanted no land from China—only trade.

In 1878, the Hayes administration sent Commodore Robert W. Shufeldt and the USS *Ticonderoga* on a voyage around the world to show the flag and explore the potential for expanded U.S. trade. He was to visit Korea—technically an independent kingdom, but actually a Chinese satellite. Shufeldt arrived in the Far East in 1880, first visiting Japan, where his intention to go on to Korea stirred opposition. Treating Korea as an independent country, the Japanese government intended to absorb it into its planned empire on the Asian mainland.

Shufeldt visited Korea anyway before returning to the United States and reporting to the new Garfield administration. Secretary of State Blaine was determined to increase the influence and prestige of the United States overseas, and Shufeldt was sent back to the Far East. Understanding that he risked being caught in the crossfire between China and Japan over Korea, Shufeldt visited both countries before securing China's approval in April 1882 of an American-Korean treaty. In May, the Koreans signed it. Americans now could live in Korea and engage in trade, but American Christian missionaries were to stay out of the Korean interior. The Arthur administration grumbled at the Chinese claims of sovereignty over Korea but approved, considering the treaty overall in the interest of the United States.[16]

Still, the United States continued to treat Korea as an independent country. In February 1883, the Arthur administration backed up its conviction by appointing Lucius H. Foote, a veteran diplomat, as minister plenipotentiary, at that time the highest foreign service rank. He was well received by the Korean government.[17]

The American minister to China, John Russell Young, a veteran journalist and the biographer of Grant, had arrived there in August 1882, ably handling relations in the wake of U.S. restrictions on Chinese immigration. While China's resentment of foreign influence was growing, its government appreciated that the United States did not occupy or seek its territory. Still, China's decline would continue as foreign, especially Japanese and Russian, incursions on its territory increased.

The Middle East

American involvement in the Middle East was limited but developing as American economic power grew. In 1883, the Persian government appealed to the Arthur administration for assistance in resisting the encroachment of the British from the south and the Russians from the north. Concerned about the safety of Christian missionaries should order break down, the president sent the United States' first official mission to Persia, led by Samuel Green Wheeler Benjamin—a painter, art historian, and journalist.

As the Americans neared Teheran, Benjamin wrote, they were met by an impressive entourage of six governors and a thousand cavalry in brilliant European-style uniforms with "touches of oriental splendor."[18] The Shah, Naser al-Din, wore a coat buttoned with diamonds "fully the size of pigeon's eggs."[19]

In return for American weapons, especially Gatling guns, the Persians offered to trade iron, coal, copper, sulphur, and agricultural products. The United States, concerned for the safety of its missionaries and intending to assert itself without challenging the major empires, had no interest in getting caught between Britain and Russia. Persia, now Iran, would continue well into the twentieth century as a zone of conflict between Britain and Russia and later between the United States and the Soviet Union.

CHAPTER 14

Society

Christian influence spread in the United States during the second half of the nineteenth century. Rod Dreher noted that during these years the United States, like England, enjoyed a revival of "a popular Christianity that was muscular, moralistic, and disciplined," as well as "notably civic-minded."[1] Changes in societal standards as well as in personal lives were marked as the revival spread and sank roots. Most Americans identified with one of the Protestant churches. The dominant denominations in the earlier years of American history—the Episcopal, Congregational, and Presbyterian churches—remained strong, but Methodist and Baptist membership had passed them because of more effective outreach as the population expanded westward. They were quicker to send people there to evangelize, and then to organize and lead new congregations.

Evangelical Christianity

The most prominent Protestant of the late nineteenth century was the evangelist Dwight Lyman Moody (1837–1899). After achieving

success as a shoe salesman, he turned his attention to Christian ministries. He was a leader in the Young Men's Christian Association (YMCA)
and in the establishment of Sunday schools. His primary ministry,
though, was leading people to a saving knowledge of Christ and subse-
quently reinforcing Christian influence in society. Moody saw societal
sin as rising out of individual sin, not the reverse. His approach was calm
and simple, rejecting both theatrics and the aura of learned depth. To
further this ministry, he founded Moody Publishers and the Moody Bible
Institute. During these years, the missionary imperative was powerful
with extensive efforts by denominational agencies and by interdenomi-
national agencies such as the Africa Inland Mission. Underlying all was
a sense of commitment to a Christian, essentially Protestant, America.
This belief was not mandated by government, but it was the most powerful societal influence—challenged, but dominant.

Serving with Moody's ministry for a short time was Cyrus Scofield
(1843–1921), a lawyer, state legislator in Kansas, and a United States
attorney. After Moody led him to Christ, Scofield became a Congregationalist minister. Then, after seeing the Biblical roots of that church
weakened, Scofield transferred to a Presbyterian ministry. He is best
known for the Scofield Reference Bible, first published in 1909 and still
influential with many evangelical and fundamentalist Protestants.

One of Moody's enthusiastic supporters was John D. Rockefeller, a
devout Baptist and Sunday school superintendent. His economic power
would peak later, but already by the Arthur years in the White House it
was significant. Rockefeller explained the connection between his faith
and his business simply: "I believe it is a religious duty to get all the
money you can, fairly and honestly; to keep all you can, and to give away
all you can."[2]

Russell Conwell (1843–1925) graduated from Yale, served as an
army officer during the Civil War, then became a lawyer. An active
Republican, he wrote campaign biographies of Grant, Hayes, Garfield,
and Blaine. After accepting Christ as Savior and Lord, he was ordained
as a Baptist minister, served as pastor of Grace Baptist Church in

Philadelphia, and founded Temple College, now Temple University, to offer evening higher educational programs for working-class people wanting to rise. When Temple became a state-funded institution in the 1960s, its Conwell School of Theology moved to Massachusetts and merged with Gordon Divinity School to form Gordon-Conwell Theological Seminary.

In his famous lecture "Acres of Diamonds," which he delivered more than six thousand times between 1873 and 1924, Conwell proclaimed, "To secure wealth is an honorable ambition, and is one great test of a person's usefulness to others.... I say, get rich, get rich! But get money honestly, or it will be a withering curse."[3] Conwell strove to ensure a Christian foundation for America's capitalist and increasingly industrial society. He believed that the wealthy were stewards of the riches entrusted to them, but he was concerned that an aristocracy of wealth could undermine the country's principles.

The Salvation Army, founded in England by William Booth (1829–1912), came to the United States in 1880. The organization sought to minister spiritually by leading people to Christ and materially through, for example, opening shelters for the homeless, day nurseries for working people, orphanages, and maternity hospitals. It was organized along military lines, with commissioned officers being ordained clergy.[4]

By the middle of the nineteenth century, liberal theology dominated a number of the colleges and universities founded by Protestant denominations, but most still were evangelical. By the 1880s, however, most of America's historically Protestant universities were liberalized.

The most notable writer of Christian hymns during the second half of the nineteenth century was Fanny Crosby (1820–1915). Blinded in infancy by the mistreatment of an eye inflammation, she never expressed bitterness at her state and developed phenomenal mental capabilities, memorizing, for example, the four Gospels and the first five books of the Old Testament.[5] Most of her hymns were written by the end of the 1870s. Among the best known and loved are "To God Be the Glory" (1875), "Blessed Assurance" (1873), "Rescue the Perishing" (1870), and

"All the Way My Savior Leads Me" (1875). Perhaps the most popular of her hymns during the 1870s through the end of the century was "Safe in the Arms of Jesus," which was used widely as part of the commemoration and mourning when Presidents Garfield and Grant died.[6]

The biggest name in the writing of novels during the 1880s was Lew Wallace (1827–1905). His *Ben-Hur: A Tale of the Christ* was published in 1880 and rapidly became a bestseller, topped only by Harriet Beecher Stowe's *Uncle Tom's Cabin* among nineteenth-century American novels. It was made into a motion picture twice in the twentieth century.

Wallace, an attorney, joined the army when the war with Mexico broke out in 1846. He again joined the army at the start of the Civil War, distinguishing himself in the capture of Fort Donelson in March 1862 and earning a promotion from brigadier general to major general. His performance at Shiloh a few weeks later was criticized as dilatory, costing him command for a short time. Restored by Lincoln, he ably defended Cincinnati against a Confederate raid and again distinguished himself in July 1864 by blocking a Confederate assault on Washington, D.C. He did well as a general, although he was off center stage when the major, most dramatic clashes took place.

His historical novel *The Fair God*, based on the Spanish invasion of Mexico under Hernán Cortés, was well received when it was published in 1873, but the success of *Ben-Hur* in the 1880s would lift Wallace to the top rank of writers. Garfield appointed him the American minister to the Ottoman Empire in 1881, a post he continued to hold through Arthur's administration.

Roman Catholicism

The Roman Catholic Church likewise grew rapidly in America in the middle and later years of the century, fed by immigration from Ireland and then from southern and eastern Europe. The first Catholics in the British North American colonies settled in Maryland in 1632. In 1790, John Carroll was consecrated bishop of Baltimore, presiding over the forty thousand Catholics in the new United States. The next year, he founded Georgetown College, the first Catholic institution of higher learning in this country. Membership in the Church grew from about 500,000 in 1830 to 3,103,000 in 1860—years when the overall population of the country increased from 12,000,000 to 31,500,000. By 1850, the Roman Catholic Church had become the single largest Christian denomination in the United States,[7] although Catholics were still a small minority in an overwhelmingly Protestant nation.[8] Prior to 1890, the U.S. census did not take note of denominational membership. According to census data, the Catholic population in 1895 was just over eight million.[9]

A number of Catholic colleges and universities had been established prior to the Civil War, such as the University of Notre Dame in Indiana, founded in 1842. In the decades after the war, the Catholic Church, concerned that most public schools were too infused with Protestant influence or were too secular, established an extensive system of Catholic elementary and secondary schools. In 1884, American Catholic bishops required all parishes to have elementary schools—even if building schools had to take precedence over building churches.[10] Growing Catholic numbers and financial resources now permitted them to take this action in a free country such as the United States.

In 1882, Father Michael J. McGivney founded the Knights of Columbus to support Roman Catholic families, especially by providing insurance. The Knights grew rapidly into an important charitable, educational, and fraternal organization,[11] providing lay Catholics with opportunities for leadership and a means for carrying out good works not just in the Church, but also in the larger community.

In the later decades of the nineteenth century, U.S. Catholic leaders pushed for the church to become more an integral part of this country and less an enclave of European culture. Probably the most significant of them was James Cardinal Gibbons, the archbishop of Baltimore, who was determined to foster the assimilation of Catholic immigrants into American society and to avoid condemning and clashing with

Protestants. Advocating the same policy was Archbishop John Ireland of St. Paul, Minnesota, who insisted, "There is no conflict between the Catholic Church and America.... The principles of the Church are in harmony with the interests of the Republic."[12]

On June 29, 1881, Pope Leo XIII set forth the Church's position in the encyclical letter *Diuturnum illud*. Different forms of government, he stated, could be accommodated legitimately, but he condemned the democratic principle that all power comes from the people, who delegate it to the government: "But as regards political power, the Church rightly teaches that it comes from God."[13]

In November 1885, several months after Arthur left the White House, the same pope, responding to new restrictions on the church in Germany and France, issued another encyclical, *Immortale Dei*, in which he affirmed:

> God alone is the true and supreme Lord of the world. Every-thing, without exception, must be subject to Him, and must serve Him, so that whosoever holds the right to govern, holds it from one sole and single source, namely God; the Sovereign Ruler of all. "There is no power but from God." Romans 13:1.[14]

In the same encyclical, he further averred, "To wish the Church to be subject to the civil power in the exercise of her duty [with respect to the supernatural order] is a great folly and a sheer injustice. When-ever this is the case, order is disturbed, for things natural are put above things supernatural."[15]

In the United States, the policies of Gibbons and Ireland prevailed, and American Catholics maintained their faith but became more and more integrated into the mainstream of American life.

Christmas

These last decades of the nineteenth century were the time when many of the familiar adjuncts to Christmas took root here. The Puritans, who had been among North America's earliest settlers and whose influence on American culture was profound, rejected celebrating the day, finding in the Bible no mention of the date of Christ's birth and reacting against the raucous celebrations common in England and in Europe. The focus on the significance of Christ's birth and the moderation of Christmas festivities led to the proclamation of the day as a national holiday in 1870. The Christmas tree came to America with German immigrants and caught on. The sending of Christmas cards came from England, and this too became popular.[16]

Santa Claus became increasingly popular during these years. The name comes from "Sinterklaas," the Dutch name for St. Nicholas, a fourth-century bishop of Myra in what today is western Turkey. Nicholas became famous and revered for his acts of charity, especially toward children.[17] Perhaps the most famous poem on Christmas is "A Visit from St. Nicholas" by Clement Clarke Moore, which was first printed in 1823:

> 'Twas the night before Christmas,
> When all through the house
> Not a creature was stirring, not even a mouse;
> The stockings were hung by the chimney with care,
> In hopes that St. Nicholas soon would be there.[18]

Thus the celebration of Christmas grew in American culture. To be sure, there was a commercial side with gifts and decorations, but the crassness of earlier festivals was reduced as the church and family aspects strengthened.

The Social Gospel

A religious movement that originated in Germany and penetrated American Protestantism in the 1880s, the "Social Gospel," sought to alter the spiritual foundation of American culture. Its praiseworthy mission was improving the lives of people here on earth with better housing, higher wages, increased educational opportunities, and expanded medical care. But the Social Gospel was aligned with the broader Progressive Era, and its focus on the spiritual soon gave way to political activism, which its supporters believed would improve both society and individual morality.

Prominent in this movement was Washington Gladden (1836–1918), a Congregationalist minister from Massachusetts who moved away from the belief in scriptural infallibility and adhered to the "higher criticism" school of interpretation, which considers the Bible primarily as a work of the human imagination. Gladden further questioned the doctrines of atonement and eternal punishment and rejected the biblical creation account, affirming evolution from species to species. His fellow liberal theologian Henry Ward Beecher (1813–1887) stated that evolution is "God's way of doing things."[19] Gladden, along with his fellow adherents to the Social Gospel, called for more government involvement in society; he rejected socialism and saw government-regulated capitalism as his ideal.

Also propounding this retreat from biblical Christianity was Horace Bushnell (1808–1876), a Yale-educated Congregational pastor in Hartford, Connecticut, who was dismayed by a revival of traditional theology in his congregation. Opposing the imposition of any orthodox creed, he sought to bridge the gulf between biblical Christianity and Unitarianism by defining the Trinity in such a way as to be acceptable to both.

Judaism

The first Jews to settle in what is now the United States arrived in New Amsterdam, now New York, in 1654. Their numbers grew slowly through the colonial years and into the first century of American independence, and though they encountered some prejudice, they were able to become integrated into American society to a degree that had been impossible in other lands—especially in Eastern Europe. In the well-known lines of President Washington's letter to the congregation of the Touro Synagogue in Newport, Rhode Island:

It is now no more that toleration is spoken of, as if it was by the indulgence of one class of people, that another enjoyed the exercise of their inherent rights. For happily the government of the United States, which gives to bigotry no sanction, to persecution no assistance, requires only that they who live under its protection should demean themselves as good citizens, in giving it on all occasions their effectual support.[20]

Between 1830 and 1840, the Jewish population in the United States grew from three thousand to fifteen thousand. From 1840 to 1850, the pace increased, bringing the total to 150,000, and by 1877 up to 250,000.[21] The greatest surge in Jewish immigration began during Arthur's presidency and followed the assassination of Tsar Alexander I in 1881, which led, irrationally and unjustly, to another outbreak of anti-Jewish persecution in Russia and in Russian-ruled areas of Eastern Europe. Between 1880 and 1900, about one-third of the Jews in Europe, some half a million, immigrated to America. These immigrants, by and large, were more observant and more determined to preserve their Judaism than the Jews who came from northern Europe.[22]

Darwin's Challenge

A serious challenge to biblical Christianity came from Charles Darwin (1809–1882). In *The Origin of Species* (1859) and *The Descent of Man* (1871), Darwin countered the biblical teaching that God is the Creator and Sustainer of all life. His thought reflected the conviction that the God who revealed the Bible is not a reality, and so there is no divine purpose to life. Darwin believed that an evolutionary process produced human beings who are free to determine their fates and improve conditions as they better understand this reality. Expanding upon Darwin's work were Herbert Spencer (1820–1903) and Thomas Huxley (1825–1895), who also considered Christianity outdated and primitive—an inadequate explanation of life. The conflict is still with us.

The influence of this philosophy on society was pernicious. Its adherents believed that human beings are basically good and that improvements will come through more education and a more powerful government run by the educated elite. Rejected was the biblical teaching that human nature, inherently sinful, can be and should be changed through Christian belief. The thoughts of these men spread from the intellectual study to the classroom, the pulpit, and finally to the political arena, strengthening the conviction that more taxation and spending would produce a better world. By no means, though, did Arthur and his government fall into this camp, and most Americans likewise rejected big government as the solution for societal problems.

The New Englander John Fiske (1842–1901), a historian and philosopher, attempted to reconcile Christianity and evolution. He saw no conflict between them, believing that God directed evolution. He rejected Darwin's rejection of God while seeing openings in Herbert Spencer's writings for putting a veneer of faith over evolution. He presented his positions quite thoroughly in his two-volume study *Outlines of Cosmic Philosophy*, which was published in 1874.[23]

Better known than Fiske was Benjamin B. Warfield (1851–1921), who graduated from the College of New Jersey, now Princeton University, in 1871 and from Princeton Theological Seminary in 1876. He served briefly in a Presbyterian pastoral ministry, then entered teaching and spent most of his career in the field back at Princeton Theological Seminary. He espoused the Bible as revelation, affirming in 1881, "The Scriptures not only contain, but ARE THE WORD OF GOD, and hence…all the elements all these affirmations are absolutely errorless, and binding on the faith and obedience of men."[24]

Warfield, though, did attempt to reconcile traditional Christian beliefs concerning the inspiration of Scripture with evolution and higher criticism, believing that God created everything in nature, including human beings, but willing to accept Darwin's scientific theories. He came to affirm that there is nothing in the Bible "that need be opposed to evolution."[25]

Also seeking to reconcile Christianity and evolution was William Graham Sumner (1840–1910), an Episcopal priest of the "Broad Church" tradition and liberal theological views who eventually left the ministry and, at Yale, became the nation's first professor of sociology. Sumner defended the gold standard and *laissez-faire* capitalism while criticizing big business for its support of government-sponsored monopolies and high tariffs. In his book *What Social Classes Owe to Each Other* (1883), Sumner attacked the "ecclesiastical prejudice in favor of the poor and against the rich."[26] His combination of liberal religious views and conservative economics has been rather uncommon in American history, though, Barry Goldwater could be said to have embodied the same combination. More common today are those who are conservative in both categories or who are liberal in both.

Marxism and Atheism

More radical in his rejection of Christianity, along with the social and economic underpinnings of Western civilization, was Karl Marx (1818–1883). During the middle and later years of the nineteenth century, the violent revolutionary action he advocated was beginning to challenge European governments, although without success. His two major works were the short *Communist Manifesto*, published in 1848, and *Capital*, often referred to by its German title, *Das Kapital*—a ponderous tome that was published in 1867.

The *Communist Manifesto*, aimed at stirring revolution, opens with the famous line: "A specter is haunting Europe—the specter of Communism."[27] A few lines later are other words equally well-known: "The history of all hitherto existing society is the history of class struggles."[28] Marx contended that the record of exploitation of the proletariat—the working class—by the bourgeoisie—the capitalist middle class—would continue until the proletariat completed its revolution, exterminated the capitalists and capitalism, and brought in the perfect society. "The Communists disdain to conceal their views and aims. They openly declare that their ends can be attained only by the forcible overthrow of all existing social conditions."[29]

Marx mistakenly believed that the advanced countries of Western Europe and the United States would be the places where communism would first succeed. He expected capitalism to become more oppressive as wealth was concentrated in fewer hands and more people fell into desperate poverty. He turned out to be completely wrong. In the United States, people with ambition and talent could rise from the socioeconomic level into which they were born. During the Arthur years, the Marxists burrowed away but made little progress.

Determined to extirpate religious influence from the United States was the National Liberal League, which had planned to contest the 1880 presidential race with the National Liberal Party and a ticket headed by the notorious agnostic Robert G. Ingersoll (1833–1899). An attorney, he served as a cavalry colonel in the Civil War, was attorney general of Illinois, and supported James G. Blaine's unsuccessful presidential run in 1876. Ingersoll vigorously attacked Christian beliefs.[30] His running mate was Francis Collingwood Abbott, who had proclaimed that he was "not only not a Christian, but also…a determined anti-Christian, aye, to the very bone."[31] The party fell apart and was not a factor in 1880. In 1885, the National Liberal League split with the more militant freethinkers and reorganized as the American Secular Union.[32]

These devotees of a society free from the influence of organized religion failed to win victory for their cause. The unofficial Christian establishment continued in the United States through the Arthur years and beyond.

Urbanization, Railroads, and Regulation

The percentage of Americans living in cities, which had been increasing throughout the nineteenth century, surged between 1870 and 1900. In those three decades, the population of the country shot from thirty-nine million to seventy-six million, while the percentage living in urban environs shot from 25 percent up to almost 40 percent. The number of cities with more than one hundred thousand inhabitants rose from twenty-four to thirty-eight. Over that same thirty-year span, Detroit's population rose from eighty thousand to 286,000, and Los Angeles grew from six thousand to more than one hundred thousand. About one-third of the increase came from immigration; the rest came from reproductive growth by the domestic population.[33]

Pullman, Illinois, represented a new kind of urban settlement—the company town. Part of Chicago today, the town was established in 1880 by George Pullman, who had grown rich in Colorado in the early 1860s. After moving to Chicago, he secured a patent on a passenger rail car that converted into a sleeper. By 1880, Pullman cars were used on sixty thousand miles of track—almost two-thirds of America's railroad lines.[34]

Pullman's company town was developed on four thousand acres bordering Lake Calumet. Single-family homes and row houses were built along tree-lined streets.[35] The community had churches, a hotel, a shopping arcade, a theater, a bank, and a library to which Pullman donated five thousand volumes. The homes, however, could not be purchased, only rented, and Pullman controlled the local government, appointing municipal officials. And residents were required to shop in company stores, where prices were higher than in stores outside the community. The population of Pullman peaked in 1885 with 8,600 residents.[36]

The company was hit by relatively minor strikes in 1884 and 1886, but neither could gain traction. Far more serious were the events of 1893–1894. The Panic of 1893 led the Pullman Company to reduce wages by an average of twenty-five percent without, however, any reduction in the rent paid by the employees or in the prices charged in the company stores. Aggravating its employees' resentment, the company did not reduce executive compensation and did not pay dividends. By early 1894, Pullman's workforce had shrunk by one-third. Many of the remaining workers gave up on Samuel Gompers's American Federation of Labor, which believed that labor and management could work together, and turned to the American Railway Union, headed by Eugene Debs, who became a five-time candidate for president on the socialist ticket.

A strike ensued in June, backed by Debs's union, which refused to operate any trains with Pullman sleeping cars. When violence erupted, the strikers lost public support, and part of organized labor even turned against them. When the strike ended and the company reopened in August 1894, workers were rehired if they left Debs's union. The use of Pullman cars continued to expand, but Pullman himself lost much public support because of his authoritarian streak.[37] He died in 1897.

Accompanying the labor unrest was a movement to regulate the railroads. Between 1874 and 1885, more than thirty bills were introduced in Congress to bring about some control of their activities, though with limited effect. Serious regulatory reform would not come until early in the next century. By the 1890s, most railroads were part of six systems, four of them controlled by J. P. Morgan.[38] The slowly growing sentiment for reform led to the establishment in 1887 of the Interstate Commerce Commission. Opposition to railroad rate discrimination—the practice of favoring some users over others, especially those shipping large quantities long distances—was key to support for this change. The Interstate Commerce Act opened the door for further involvement by the government. Then, as well as today and always, free societies have to find the balance between the Scylla of regulating so much that freedom is strangled and the Charybdis of having so little oversight that either chaotic disintegration ensues or a few powerful people dominate everything.

The Temperance Movement

The temperance movement grew impressively during the second half of the nineteenth century. In 1851, Maine became the first state to ban the sale of alcoholic beverages. More states moved to do the same in the 1880s, although—as related earlier—without the support of Chester Arthur. The impetus came primarily from women, especially Christian women. Of prime significance in the rise of prohibition was Frances

Willard (1839–1898), a Methodist and a teacher who headed the Women's Christian Temperance Union, which had started in 1874. She later moved on to espouse other interests, and her eventual involvement with Christian socialism diminished her influence. Literary figures aided the temperance drive with books such as Stephen Crane's *Maggie: A Girl of the Streets* (1893) and Upton Sinclair's *The Jungle* (1906), which brought attention to the destructive power of alcohol. The consumption of alcohol in the United States did drop from the first three decades of the century to the last three decades.[39]

The Prohibition Party won a few races in a few states but never became a major political force, peaking with slightly more than 2 percent of the popular vote for president in 1892. The drive to outlaw alcoholic beverages gained momentum during these last decades of the nineteenth century and into the opening years of the twentieth, culminating with the overwhelming approval by Congress of the Eighteenth Amendment to the United States Constitution in 1917. The vote in Congress—140 Democrats and 138 Republicans in favor of prohibition, sixty-four Democrats and sixty-two Republicans opposed—showed that both support and opposition crossed party lines. The amendment was ratified January 16, 1919. Support would fade, and in less than a decade and a half national prohibition was repealed by the Twenty-first Amendment. For a few more years, it would remain in some states and municipalities.

Henry George

Presenting a rather singular economic position during the 1880s was Henry George (1839–1897). Born and raised in Philadelphia, he prospected for gold, without success, in British Columbia and became a successful journalist in San Francisco, rising to be managing editor of the *San Francisco Times*. He came to oppose private land ownership, publishing his views in 1879 in *Progress and Poverty: An Inquiry into the Causes of Industrial Depressions and of Increase of Want with*

Increase of Wealth. The book sold briskly, bringing him income, fame, and political opportunities. George believed that land was concentrated in the hands of too few and that the owners benefitted from population growth and other factors that were not the product of their effort. Land, he argued, should be owned not individually, but collectively. Users would pay rent, which would permit all other forms of taxation to be abolished.[40]

In 1886, George challenged the two major parties with his campaign for mayor of New York. His opponents were Democrat U.S. representative Abram S. Hewitt and Republican Theodore Roosevelt. After an exciting and hard-fought campaign, Hewitt won with 90,552 votes, followed by George with 68,110 and Roosevelt with 60,435.[41] Needless to say, Roosevelt was chagrined to finish third, but clearly thousands of Republicans supported Hewitt because of their horror at the prospect of Henry George as mayor. In New York City in 1885, Hewitt was going to win, but without the fear of George, the vote would have been closer. Soon to fade from prominence, George stirred both opposition and hope in the 1870s and 1880s.

Getting from Here to There

In the 1880s, the automobile moved from dream to reality. The concept of a self-propelled land vehicle had occurred to the ancient Greeks, but they did not advance beyond theoretical knowledge. In 1769, the Frenchman Nicolas-Joseph Cugnot made a three-wheeled cart with a boiler powering a two-cylinder steam engine, which drove the front wheel—the first true automobile. In 1801, the Cornishman Richard Trevithick built a four-wheeled steam vehicle. And in 1804, the American Oliver Evans put wheels on a boat and drove it.[42] Throughout these decades, the development of automobiles was hampered by competition from faster and smoother railroads, the paucity of roads with good surfaces, and a want of financial backing. By the 1880s, however, these conditions were changing.

In 1879, George Selden, an American attorney and promoter, applied for a patent for a car with a gasoline-powered engine, but he never completed the prototype. The first patent awarded for a gasoline-powered automobile went to Karl Benz of Germany on January 29, 1886, although he had been producing vehicles since 1883. In the United States, Ransom Olds was building gasoline engines by 1885, and in 1887 he drove his steam vehicle in Lansing, Michigan.[43]

Since Europe had more good roads than the United States, it led in the development of the automobile. But that would change. By the early years of the twentieth century, American road construction had boomed, and its automobile industry had moved to the top.

Railroads expanded dramatically in last three decades of the nineteenth century, surging from 46,844 miles of track to 193,346. On May 10, 1869, the first transcontinental rail line was completed when crews building from the east and those coming from the west met at Promontory Point, Utah. By 1884, three more rail lines crossed the country: the Northern Pacific ran from Lake Superior to Portland, Oregon; the Southern Pacific extended from New Orleans to Los Angeles and then north to San Francisco; the Santa Fe started in Atchison, Kansas, then passed through Colorado and New Mexico to San Diego.[44] This expansion opened up vast areas in the middle and western parts of the country to development, spurring population and economic growth.

As the railroad network spread, new parts of the country developed, thanks to the greater ease for people to move there and the boost in commercial activity now possible. During the forty years from 1870 to 1910, average railroad freight rates fell from 2.7 cents per ton mile to 0.75 cents and passenger rates declined from 2.8 cents per passenger mile to 1.9 cents.[45] Still, there were complaints that big, long-distance shippers received price breaks from the railroads. The railroad management responded that this was standard business practice. A further complicating factor was that increasing competition between railroad companies in the same territory became less profitable because of the expense for each to lay track and build bridges, for example. This declining competition, dependence on the railroads, and the reality that these companies received extensive land grants from the federal government to spur their building into sparsely populated areas led to the slow but steady growth in government regulation.

A few years before Arthur became president, the theatrical impresario Henry C. Jarrett, in cooperation with the *New York Herald*, promoted an assault on the record for crossing the United States from coast to coast. His special train left New York at 12:40 a.m. on June 1, 1876, and arrived in Oakland, California, one minute short of eighty-four hours later—an achievement that stirred enthusiasm for pushing the limits on what could be known and what could be done. These latter years of the nineteenth century were remarkable for their innovation and dynamic growth.

The Closing of the Frontier

Rapidity of communication also increased in the years after the Civil War. Samuel Morse had developed the first telegraph in 1837. By the time of Arthur, it was well developed. On March 10, 1876, Alexander Graham Bell spoke over a telephone for the first time. Two years later, in 1878, the first switchboard went into operation and usage spread rapidly.

These advances in travel and communication helped bring about the closing of the American frontier. In 1890, the Census Bureau would declare that no frontier remained within the United States. There still were sparsely populated regions, but the days of the frontier were past. In 1884, as President Arthur neared the end of his term, Frederick Jackson Turner (1861–1932) graduated from the University of Wisconsin. He came to see the frontier as a safety valve, an arena in which capable people who lacked the advantages of birth and education could fulfill their ambitions. In the East, it was possible for people to climb the social and economic ladder, starting from the bottom, as Andrew Carnegie had done, but in the West, the rise was more rapid, with a greater element of adventure added. That sense of adventure drew people from upper-class and upper-middle-class backgrounds, such as Theodore Roosevelt. Turner presented his views in a lecture, "The Significance of the Frontier in American History," to the American Historical Association on July 12, 1893. He saw the closing of the frontier as the ending of a great historical period in the development of the United States, but he believed American dynamism would be refocused on new areas.[46] He was right, although as a progressive Democrat and an admirer of William Jennings Bryan and Woodrow Wilson, he would not always be happy with where the focus was.

Yellowstone National Park, established in 1872, is the oldest national park in the world. In March 1883, Senator George Vest of Missouri, a former Confederate senator and representative, took steps to stop development of Yellowstone, ensuring its continuation in its natural state for future generations. In August of that year, Arthur became the first president to visit the park. He supported conservation in general, that of Yellowstone especially. Furthering the cause of keeping the park as an undeveloped treasure, Congress blocked the attempts of the Northern Pacific Railroad to build spur lines into it.[47]

Americans' perennial fascination with the West was behind the success of William "Buffalo Bill" Cody's Wild West show, which began in 1883. Cody (1846–1917), a Pony Express rider in 1860, fought with the Kansas volunteer cavalry in the Civil War. After the war, he became a successful buffalo hunter, earning his nickname, but achieved more fame as a civilian scout with the army fighting the Indians. In 1872, he was awarded the Medal of Honor for his heroism during an action in Nebraska.[48] During Arthur's presidency, Cody's Wild West show achieved great success, becoming popular in the United States and overseas.[49]

Sports

The tradition of the seventh-inning stretch traces originated in a baseball game in 1882 between Manhattan College, a Roman Catholic institution in New York, and a semi-pro team called the Metropolitans. Brother Jasper, the athletic director at Manhattan, called a timeout during the seventh inning to give students a chance to stand and stretch together.[50]

During Arthur's presidency, baseball was developing as a popular game and a thriving business. It emerged as a serious professional sport in 1871 when nine teams established the National Association of Professional Base Ball Players. (The words "base" and "ball" were not combined in the sport's name until the next century.) The first night baseball game was played a few years later, on September 2, 1880, when teams representing two Boston stores, Jordan Marsh and R. H. White, met under the lights in Hull, Massachusetts. Thirty-six lamps on three towers were powered by two engines and three generators.[51]

By 1881, the year Arthur became the third president in less than seven months, the National League comprised the Chicago White Stockings, the Providence Grays, the Buffalo Bisons, the Detroit Wolverines, the Troy Trojans, the Boston Red Caps, the Cleveland Blues, and the Worcester Ruby Legs.

The next year, the National League was challenged by the six-team American Association: the Cincinnati Red Stockings, the Philadelphia Athletics, the Louisville Eclipse, the Pittsburgh Alleghenys, the St. Louis Browns, and the Baltimore Orioles.[52] The league folded after the 1891 season. In 1901, the American League was formed and the present two leagues began their rivalry.

Football, too, was emerging as a major spectator sport during the late nineteenth century, developing from the English game of rugby. In 1875, Harvard defeated Yale in what is considered the first game of American football. The most important person in these early years was Walter Camp (1859–1925), a multi-sport athlete at Yale and the brother-in-law of William Graham Sumner. Although he had a career in business,

Camp was the key factor in Yale football from 1876 to 1909, sometimes as the paid official coach, generally more informally as an advisor.[53]

Professional football was slower to develop than professional baseball. Although there are reports that a player was paid for a game in 1892, the sport was not significant as a profession until the start of the National Football League in 1920.

Professional boxing emerged from the shadows during the 1880s, made popular by John L. Sullivan. In earlier years, boxing was frowned upon and usually illegal. On February 7, 1882, Sullivan knocked out Paddy Ryan in the ninth round and claimed the heavyweight championship of the United States. He later was acknowledged as the world champion, reigning until September 7, 1892, when James J. Corbett defeated him. During his years as the heavyweight title holder, Sullivan became world-famous and rich. To him goes the credit for establishing boxing as a legitimate sport that would flourish in the twentieth century.[54]

Lawn tennis had begun in the United States in 1874, followed a few years later by golf. Each, though, was primarily a sport for the well-to-do. Their spread to a wider range of Americans lay several decades in the future.

The American Indian game of lacrosse had been picked up by Canadians of European ancestry and spread to the United States in the years after the Civil War. In 1879, eleven teams in New York, Massachusetts, and Pennsylvania formed the United States National Amateur Lacrosse Association. Colleges then picked up on the sport and in 1883 established the Intercollegiate Association, which included such notable institutions as Harvard, Yale, Princeton, and Lehigh.[55] Although the game did spread and is still played, it did not attract a broad base of support, remaining a sport "germinated in private athletic clubs as well as prestigious institutions of higher and secondary education."[56]

The Arts and Entertainment

A cultural milestone of the 1880s was the opening of the Metropolitan Opera Company in New York City on October 22, 1883, with a performance of *Faust* followed two days later by *Lucia di Lammermoor*.[57] From the beginning it was one of the premier opera companies in the world, a position it holds to this day. Performances were held in the famed Metropolitan Opera House at Thirty-ninth and Broadway until the company moved to its new location at the Lincoln Center in 1966.

The Boston Symphony Orchestra was founded in 1881, joining the already flourishing New York Philharmonic and followed within a few years by symphony orchestras in Philadelphia, Chicago, Cincinnati, and other cities.

American composers too were rising in acclaim during these last two decades of the nineteenth century. Edward MacDowell (1861–1908) was acclaimed as the greatest American composer of this period. Victor Herbert and Reginald De Koven wrote successful operettas following the lead of Englishmen W. S. Gilbert and Arthur Sullivan.[58]

American painters also contributed to their country's growing artistic reputation. By the late 1850s, Winslow Homer (1836–1910) was beginning to make his mark with illustrations for *Harper's Weekly*. By the late 1870s he had moved into painting seascapes. Soon he moved to Prouts Neck, Maine, where he settled and painted the seascapes for which he is most famous. By the end of the century, he reigned as the premier American painter, highly regarded internationally. Joining him at the top of American artists were his younger contemporaries John Singer Sargent (1856–1925) and James Abbott McNeill Whistler (1834–1903).[59]

The 1880s saw the waning of the Hudson River School of painting, the first indigenous American art movement. It had arisen in the mid-1820s and was at peak in the 1850s, 1860s, and 1870s. The scenes depicted at first were in the Hudson River region of New York; later the focus spread to other parts of the country. This marked the beginning of landscape painting in the United States. The artists were committed to expressing their Christian faith and uplifting viewers through the beauty and the inspiration of what they put on canvas. The key historian of this movement, James F. Cooper, succinctly phrased it: "They devoted their talents to the pursuit of beauty and the sacred."[60]

Phineas Taylor Barnum (1810–1891) was a premier showman and theatrical entrepreneur who brought the great Swedish soprano Jenny Lind to the United States in 1850–1851. He is best known, though, as the creator of the most successful American traveling circus. Each year it visited communities from Nova Scotia to California and crossed the Atlantic to thrill English audiences. In 1881, he combined his operation with that of James A. Bailey and James L. Hutchinson, becoming even more dominant as Barnum and Bailey.[61]

The last quarter of the nineteenth century overall was a commendable time of growth and improvement. Civic-mindedness was high with the highest voter participation in our history. Hospitals and schools increased impressively in number during this time. Furthermore, the demand grew for improving clean water supplies and for better disposing of sewage. Arthur did not create the call for reform, but he and his administration did not simply ride on the crest of this wave; they actively furthered the movement.

CHAPTER 15

1884 Election

A s 1884 opened, it was clear that Arthur lacked a solid political base. The reformers still did not see him as one of them, and the Stalwarts saw him as an apostate. Carl Schurz, a German immigrant who served as a brigadier general in the Civil War, a U.S. senator, and secretary of the interior in the Hayes administration, said that Arthur "literally sat down between two chairs."[1]

Still, Arthur enjoyed the support of certain powerful Republicans, especially Northeastern pro-business Republicans. On May 20, his enthusiastic supporters packed the Cooper Union auditorium in New York City to hear speakers from both the Reform and the Stalwart wings of the party. In a telegram read to the audience, Civil Service Commissioner Dorman B. Eaton reminded them, "President Arthur has done everything the commission has asked him to do in aid of civil service reform, which is vastly indebted to his firm and decided stand in its favor for the success it has achieved during the past year."[2] Yet to most Reform Republicans, Arthur was still a product of the Conkling machine, and they rejected his candidacy for a full term as president.

GETTING HOT ENOUGH FOR HIM.

Republican factionalism takes a toll: "Getting Hot Enough for Him"
Courtesy of the Library of Congress

Pro-business Republicans such as J. H. Herrick, the president of the New York Produce Exchange, were impressed with Arthur's economic policies and his personal integrity,[3] and they did not blame him for the deteriorating economic conditions of 1883–1884. The once-rapid expansion of the steel industry had slowed dramatically, bringing down prices and wages and increasing unemployment, and there was a wave of bank failures caused by both dishonesty and bad judgment. Still, the slump was less severe than the Panic of 1873, during Grant's presidency, and the Panic of 1893, which would bedevil Cleveland's second term.[4]

A Reluctant Candidate and the Alternatives

For reasons that are not clear, Arthur did not campaign seriously for his party's nomination in 1884. He destroyed his personal papers shortly before his death in 1886, and since he offered no explanation to any trusted associate, there is no reliable secondhand evidence. Perhaps he was constrained by the view that it was not good form for a president openly to seek the office, though past chief executives had done so. Perhaps he hoped that Blaine's strength would diminish as people learned more of him, though Blaine, a former Speaker of the House, U.S. senator, and secretary of state, was as well-known as a politician could be. The most likely explanation is medical—that Arthur knew that Bright's disease would keep him from campaigning vigorously and that he was unlikely to survive another term if he won. He did not, though, want his condition known, lest it cause insecurity and dissension.

Arthur did not admire Blaine's character and believed that he would not be a good president. He might have hoped for the emergence of an alternative to Blaine whom he could support. Blaine's brilliance and knowledge of government were beyond dispute, as was his legendary eloquence, which he wielded as a political weapon. He and Roscoe Conkling had been rivals and enemies almost from the time they first met as members of the House of Representatives in the 1860s. During a bitter debate in 1866, Blaine had mocked Conkling's "haughty disdain, his grandiloquent swell, his majestic, super-eminent, overpowering, turkey-gobbler strut."[5] Such rhetoric pleased Blaine's supporters but made him lasting enemies.

More troubling were the questions about Blaine's integrity. In Carl Schurz's vivid words, Blaine had "wallowed in the spoils like a rhinoceros in an African pool."[6] He never was convicted in a court of law, but an unsavory aroma clung to him for his involvement with companies that had government contracts. Personal enmity and concerns about his honesty kept some Republicans from endorsing Blaine, but for many others, his experience, oratory, and charisma overcame these flaws. This was not the first time voters had to weigh a candidate's impressive strengths against his apparently unsavory character, nor would it be the last.

Many Republicans were hoping that the Civil War hero William Tecumseh Sherman would run. Rather than waiting for Sherman to grow into a serious threat to his candidacy, Blaine told him in a telegram that the nomination could be his if he wanted it. The general's terse response, "I will not accept if nominated and will not serve if elected,"[7] was a classic rejection which could not have been clearer. The most serious obstacle to Blaine's nomination was gone.

Hoping for a deadlock between Arthur and Blaine were those backing Senator George Edmunds of Vermont, a man of admirable character but an uninspiring speaker. He chaired the Senate Judiciary Committee, and after Arthur succeeded Garfield, his Senate colleagues elected him president pro tempore. He had a bloc of about seventy delegates led by Theodore Roosevelt and Representative Henry Cabot Lodge of Massachusetts. These men were unconvinced that a different Chester Arthur was president, and they were horrified by the prospect of a Blaine presidency.[8]

There also was interest in Robert Todd Lincoln, primarily because of the power of his name, though he had demonstrated impressive ability in the law, in business, and in the cabinet. In January 1884, John Hay, discussing prospective contenders, mentioned "Bob Lincoln, who has no organized following but a strong though diffused sentiment for him—greatly to his annoyance as he is for Arthur."[9] Two months earlier, in December 1883, Judge S. Newton Pettis of Pennsylvania, the U.S. minister to Bolivia during the Lincoln administration, wrote of the younger Lincoln, "The Secretary declares he is in no rush for a nomination and feels somewhat embarrassed by the action of his friends in pushing him while a member of Arthur's cabinet."[10]

The Nominating Conventions of 1884

The Republican National Convention opened on June 3, 1884, in the same Chicago Exposition Building where it had met four years before to nominate the ticket of Garfield and Arthur. In 1927, a friend of Theodore Roosevelt's, President Nicholas Murray Butler of Columbia University, looked back on the 1884 convention with perhaps a dash of hyperbole as "the ablest body of men that ever came together in America since the original Constitutional Convention."[11]

The Blaine-dominated National Committee nominated General Powell Clayton for temporary chairman of the convention. A former governor of Arkansas and U.S. senator, he had a good Civil War record, but his involvement in the Star Route scandal repelled a number of Blaine backers. Lodge nominated former representative John R. Lynch of Mississippi, born a slave to a mixed-race mother and an Irish-born overseer. Having lost his seat in Congress when white Democrats regained control of Mississippi, Lynch practiced law in Washington, D.C., and later served as a major in the Spanish-American War.

The South at this time delivered no electoral votes to the Republicans, but it did account for a quarter of the delegates at the convention—mostly blacks. The combination of anti-Blaine delegates and Blaine dissidents gave Lynch a victory over Clayton, 424 to 384. Blaine's prospects endured a further blow the next day when John B. Henderson of Missouri, an Edmunds supporter, was elected permanent chairman of the convention. Anti-Blaine hopes were high, but the antipathy among the camps of the other contenders prevented them from coming together behind an alternative to Blaine, whose nomination became inevitable. There was reluctance to back Arthur, and an attempt to bring together the Arthur and Edmunds delegates in support of John Sherman broke down, some of Arthur's backers disliking Sherman more than Blaine. Even though they could not agree on someone else, those opposing Blaine were determined to have their say, reminding the delegates what a mistake choosing him would be.

Once the convention was underway, delegates who thought that none of the front-runners could win the general election began to think about Robert Lincoln. On June 2, 1884, the *New York Times* editorialized that, though Senator Edmunds was the best man, he could not win the nomination and Robert Lincoln should therefore be the Republican standard-bearer:

> What stronger name could be presented to the convention, what name more certain to secure a hearty endorsement than that of Robert T. Lincoln. Mr. Lincoln is an energetic and capable Secretary of War. His successful administration of that department gives the assurance of a creditable discharge of the duties of the Presidency. The supporters of all the other candidates, without exception, have claimed him for the second place on their tickets, showing clearly that he is entirely acceptable to every group and faction of the party and has the confidence of all Republicans. Moreover—and we consider the fact one of the prize importance—Mr. Lincoln *has no political debts*. The office would come to him unsought, and he would be absolutely free to administer the great trust without bias of any kind, personal or political. Next to the name of Edmunds, the name of Lincoln is the strongest that could be presented to the convention and to the country.[12]

Lincoln, though, remained adamant that he supported Arthur's nomination, that he would not run, and that he wanted all efforts on his behalf to cease. Again, in 1888, Lincoln had to squelch calls for him to lead the party back to the White House.

When the convention met on June 5 to nominate its presidential ticket, the first name put forward was that of Senator Joseph R. Hawley of Connecticut, a minor candidate enjoying his moment in the sun. He was nominated by former Representative Augustus Brandegee, who, obviously referring to Blaine, berated machine politics. Next presented to the delegates was Senator John Logan of Illinois, a successful Civil War general but a man as entrenched in the spoils system as Blaine was. As expected, when the name of Blaine was presented the response in the convention hall was ecstatic, swamping in size and enthusiasm other demonstrations both before and after.

Then Arthur was nominated by Martin I. Townsend, the district attorney of Troy, New York, with a rambling and tepid address. Representative Harry H. Bingham of Pennsylvania did better seconding the nomination, praising Arthur's courage and record as president. John Lynch failed to excite the delegates with his seconding speech. Patrick H. Winston of North Carolina and P. B. S. Pinchback of Louisiana did no better as they took their turns.[13]

The last candidate presented to the weary delegates was Senator Edmunds, the hope of the reformers in the party. Former governor John D. Long of Massachusetts presented him as an honest man who could unite the divided party. Finally, after midnight, the session ended.

On the morning of June 6, the voting began. Winning the nomination required 411 votes on the first ballot. Blaine led with 334½ votes, followed by Arthur with 278, Edmunds with ninety-three, Logan with sixty-three and a half, Sherman with thirty, and the remaining votes scattered. On the next two ballots there was little change; Blaine led on the second ballot with 349 votes to Arthur's 276 and on the third 375 to 274. But Blaine's strength was apparent, and his opponents were unable to coalesce around someone else. Logan, spotting an opening for himself, switched to Blaine on the fourth ballot, the result being a Blaine-Logan ticket for the November election.

Now that the convention had chosen these men, a split in the party was inevitable. Although many Republican reformers such as Theodore Roosevelt and Henry Cabot Lodge gritted their teeth and supported the ticket, others bolted and endorsed Grover Cleveland, whom the Democrats nominated the following month. Among those Republicans now working to elect Cleveland were Henry Ward Beecher, Charles Francis Adams Jr., and Carl Schurz. About the choice of Blaine, Schurz fulminated:

> Do you not see that the best Republican principles have already been defeated by that nomination? Do you not see that those principles which were the great soul of the Republican Party, command you maintain good government at any rate, be it even the timely sacrifice of party ascendency?[14]

Joining these Republicans in supporting Cleveland were such ordinarily Republican publications as the *New York Times*, the *Nation*, and *Harper's Weekly*.[15]

Arthur wired congratulations to Blaine and promised support. Two weeks later, Frank B. Conger, the son of a Stalwart senator and a key leader of the Arthur forces at the convention, met with the president at the White House and learned that he had at most two years to live.[16] Arthur's health and his disdain for Blaine kept him from actively campaigning for the ticket.

The Democrats convened in Chicago a few weeks later. Samuel Tilden's health precluded his running, but the party had no shortage of prospective standard-bearers. Senator Thomas Bayard of Delaware, who had run in 1876 and 1880, declared his candidacy, as did former Speaker of the House Samuel J. Randall of Pennsylvania, the current Speaker, John G. Carlisle of Kentucky, and former Senator Allen G. Thurman of Ohio. In case anyone should stumble, Thomas Hendricks, a former member of the U.S. House and Senate and a former governor of Indiana, a man who had tried to gain the presidential nomination three previous times, stood poised to jump in. Dark horse candidates included Governor George Hoadly of Ohio and former senator Joseph McDonald of Indiana.

Most intriguing of all was Governor Grover Cleveland of New York, whose rise had been almost too meteoric even for fiction. He won election as mayor of Buffalo in 1881, as governor of New York in 1882, and now was on the brink of the presidency. In each office, he demonstrated ability, integrity, and courage, along with a commitment to limited taxation and spending.

Nominating speeches were made on July 9 and voting began. At the time, the Democrats required a two-thirds vote for nomination, which meant 547 delegates. First-ballot results showed Cleveland clearly in first place, although well short of the two-thirds figure, with 392 votes, followed by Bayard with 170, Thurman with eighty-eight, Randall with seventy-eight, and McDonald with fifty-six. Hendricks, not a declared contender, received one vote. At one thirty in the morning, the exhausted delegates voted to adjourn for a few hours of sleep—and more scheming and maneuvering.

The next day's attempts to block Cleveland failed. When second ballot left him just seventy-two votes shy of the nomination, the opposition collapsed. State after state switched its vote to Cleveland, putting him over the top. One of his inveterate opponents, Tammany Hall, rationalized that electing him president at least would get him out of New York. Having put a proponent of the gold standard at the top of its ticket, the convention balanced that position with Hendricks, who favored an inflationary, soft-money policy.[17] Some of the support for Hendricks might have been sentimental, as he had been Tilden's running mate in that dramatic loss in 1876.

As in 1880, there were few substantial differences between the major parties in the presidential campaign of 1884. Both candidates stood for sound money and the gold standard. Neither supported high taxation and spending; neither wanted the government to increase taxes on the productive and provide more benefits for the less productive. They differed on the tariff—the Republicans advocating high rates to protect business and jobs, the Democrats arguing that low rates benefitted consumers. There were, though, attempts to roil the waters. The *New York Herald*, for example, tried to stir up voters with charges that Arthur's buildup of the navy was costly and could lead to war:

> Peace is our normal condition, and it will not be broken save by the recklessness or mad ambition of politicians. Therefore we distrust and oppose all schemes for undue increase of fortifications and of additions to the army and navy which are beyond the obvious needs of a peace establishment.... If allowed to be gratified it can only lead to increased extravagance and corruption in all branches of Government and if it should finally plunge us into war we should be the ultimate sufferers from the revival of the military regime whatever victories we might gain over foreign foes.[18]

Well to the left of both major parties stood the Greenback Labor Party, which called for paper money unbacked by either gold or silver and an income tax. Its presidential candidate was Benjamin Butler, a Civil War general who served five terms in the U.S. House of Representatives as a Republican and then was elected governor of Massachusetts as a Democrat. The party had entered the presidential contests of 1876 and 1880 and had won fourteen seats in the House in 1878. Republicans hoped that Butler would drain votes from the Democrats, while he dreamed of drawing enough electoral votes to deny victory to Blaine or Cleveland and throw the choice of the next president into the House of Representatives, where he might maneuver to his advantage. Butler did gain some newspaper support. The *New York Sun*'s part-owner and editor, Charles Dana, a Democrat, opposed Cleveland personally and hoped his endorsement of Butler would stir up controversy.

The Prohibition Party was contesting its fourth presidential election, having first entered the fray in 1872. Its presidential nominee, like the

Greenbacks', was a Civil War veteran and a former governor: John St. John, a onetime Republican who had served as a lieutenant colonel in the war and as governor of Kansas. The Prohibition Party initially attracted some people with socialist and pacifist views, and in the nineteenth century it supported women's suffrage and the direct popular election of the president. The party still exists, though its tenor is now Christian and conservative.

Campaign Scandals

In the absence of major differences in policy between the major parties, the campaign of 1884 was expected to be relatively tame. But personal problems in the backgrounds of both candidates led to a rancorous contest.

Grover Cleveland, a bachelor, had had romantic relations a decade earlier with a young Buffalo widow named Maria Halpin. So had a number of other prominent men, including, apparently, Cleveland's law partner, Oscar Folsom. In 1874, Halpin gave birth out of wedlock to a son, identifying Cleveland as the father and naming the child Oscar Folsom Cleveland. A financially successful unmarried man, Cleveland made an attractive target. He neither admitted nor denied that he was the father, but he did pay Halpin's expenses and, after learning that she was drinking heavily, arranged for the boy to be placed in an orphanage, from which he later was adopted. Folsom was killed in an accident the next year, leaving his widow and eleven-year-old daughter, Frances, well provided for financially. Cleveland served as the girl's guardian—she called him "Uncle Cleve"—but as she grew up they came to see each other in a different light. They were married in the White House during Cleveland's first term.[19]

When the story of Maria Halpin emerged during the 1884 campaign, Cleveland told his supporters, "Whatever you do, tell the truth." Some of his opponents condemned him as a debaucher of innocent women, a charge for which there was no basis. Most of the public seemed to dismiss the affair as at worst a youthful indiscretion and at best a noble sacrifice to spare the reputation of a now dead friend and his family.[20]

America's first successful humor magazine was *Puck*, published from 1876 to 1918 and named after the mischievous sprite who wittily torments the other characters in Shakespeare's *A Midsummer Night's Dream*. In its heyday of the 1880s and 1890s, its barbed prose and political cartoons targeted both Republicans and Tammany Hall—the latter dangerously dominated, in the editors' views, by Roman Catholics. *Puck* particularly despised Blaine, and its mockery contributed to his surprising loss of New York state, which cost him the presidency in 1884. The rise of William Jennings Bryan and the dramatic move of the Democrats to the left led the editors to support William McKinley in 1896 as the successor to Cleveland. *Puck*'s success inspired competition, and the magazine declined over its last two decades. William Randolph Hearst purchased it in 1917 but failed to revive it. The September 1918 issue was its last.

Blaine received support from some of the Irish Catholic press, which castigated Cleveland as a "Presbyterian bigot" and urged readers not to automatically vote for Democrats lest they be taken for granted.[21] But Blaine lost that support through inadvertence. On October 29, he met with a group of Protestant clergymen at the Fifth Avenue Hotel in Philadelphia. Speaking on behalf of those present, Reverend Dr. Samuel D. Burchard of the Murray Hill Presbyterian Church in New York City pledged their joint support to Blaine, concluding, "We are Republicans and don't propose to leave our party and identify ourselves with the party whose antecedents have been Rum, Romanism, and Rebellion."[22] The exhausted Blaine did not recognize the danger to his campaign of such sentiments. He personally was not religiously prejudiced, his mother and sister being Roman Catholic, but his failure to respond quickly cost him.

Senator Arthur Gorman of Maryland, the Democratic campaign manager, had sent a stenographer to the meeting, which was open to reporters. The Democrats quickly recognized their opportunity and widely publicized the words. There still was some gain in castigating white Democratic Southerners for the Civil War, although its effectiveness now was fading as national unity revived. Prohibition had its supporters but was not yet a winning issue nationally. There were people with anti–Roman Catholic convictions, but the Catholic vote was substantial in some states, including New York. Blaine repudiated Burchard's words the next day, but it was too late to undo the damage.[23]

Blaine, though, was not above slashing at the Democrats for the Civil War that had ended almost twenty years earlier, such as when he told a crowd in Indiana:

> The Democrats dream that they will seize the government of the nation. I do not believe that the men who added lustre and renown to your state through four years of bloody war can be used to call to the administration of the government the men who organized the great Rebellion.[24]

The same day as the Burchard stumble, Blaine added to his public relations nightmare by attending a lavish banquet at Delmonico's in New York with the tycoons Jay Gould, Andrew Carnegie, John Jacob Astor, Cyrus Field, and Henry Flagler. Walt McDougall skewered Blaine in Joseph Pulitzer's *New York World* with a cartoon depicting formally dressed plutocrats dining sumptuously while a ragged man, woman, and child begged for scraps.[25] However unfair the cartoon was to men who were constructive creators of wealth and practiced philanthropy on a vast scale, it added to Blaine's public relations headaches.

The General Election

The results of Blaine's uncharacteristic failure to spot the pitfalls before him were apparent in the results of the general election on November 4. Cleveland carried twenty states with 219 electoral votes. Blaine won eighteen states that gave him 182 electoral votes. Cleveland narrowly won the popular vote: 4,911,017 (49 percent) to 4,848,334 (48 percent). It was not a good election for third parties; the Greenback and

Prohibition Parties split the few remaining votes—175,370 votes for Butler and 150,309 for St. John.

In one state, however, the Prohibition ticket might have taken enough votes from Blaine to have cost him the election. Cleveland owed his victory to the thirty-six electoral votes of New York, which he carried by only 1,047 popular votes. The "Rum, Romanism, and Rebellion" episode aroused the antipathy of Catholic voters, especially those of Irish background, but they usually voted Democratic anyway. More costly to Blaine were the votes of 25,016 New Yorkers for the Prohibition nominee, St. John, votes that were likely to have otherwise gone to the Republican.

Blaine was weakened, especially in New York, by the resentment of his fellow Republicans. The New York Republican State Committee, controlled by supporters of Arthur, by and large stood aside from the presidential race and concentrated on assisting other party candidates. Roscoe Conkling, bitter about not getting the nomination for which he had yearned, actually worked behind the scenes to defeat Blaine.[26] The upstate New York vote was lower than usual, showing some remaining Conkling influence. The *New York Sun* commented on Blaine's loss: "It was a handful of unforgiving Stalwarts that did it."[27] The *Washington Post* also saw Conkling's fingerprints, editorializing rather archly that Democrats should "chip in and elect Mr. Conkling as a Republican Senator."[28] Actually, this was the political last gasp of a man soon to be forgotten. He died in April 1888. Finally, Reform Republicans, the "Mugwumps," preferred Cleveland to Blaine. All these factors combined for Cleveland's narrow victory in New York, which made him the first Democratic president in a generation.

For the Republicans, there were reasons for optimism in spite of the divisions caused by the Blaine candidacy. They retained control of the Senate, actually gaining one seat. The Democrats kept the control of the House, which they had won in 1882, but their margin was narrowed by the Republican gain of twenty-one seats. Republicans interpreted 1884 as a rejection of Blaine rather than a rejection of their party. In this they were correct. Blaine would continue as an important political figure, serving again as secretary of state, but his greatest power now lay behind him. For Logan, the political end would come sooner. He died December 26, 1886, remembered as a brave warrior and a skilled general but also as a spoils-loving politician.

Americans had moved through another election, imperfectly but successfully. Russell Kirk, citing Orestes Brownson, who died a few years before Arthur's presidency, stated that the providential mission of the United States "is to reconcile liberty with law."[29] To an impressive extent, the nation did that in 1884, as it had done earlier.

CHAPTER 16

The Last Act

The election was over, but Arthur still would be president until March 4. Not until 1937, after the ratification of the Twentieth Amendment, would the date of presidential inaugurations move up to January 20. The question of an American-controlled canal through Central America came to a head when the lame-duck Arthur administration signed the treaty with Nicaragua that the Senate would refuse to ratify. On January 18, 1885, the USS *Alliance* put marines ashore in Panama, then part of Colombia, to guard the American-owned railroad that crossed the isthmus against rebels. By May, the Colombian government was back in control and the marines withdrew.[1] The Arthur administration was determined to protect American interests, but Cleveland, who assumed the presidency in March, was less interested in expanding American power. Arthur was ahead of most Americans, and a canal linking the Atlantic and Pacific Oceans remained a dream until the Theodore Roosevelt years.

During these last weeks of Arthur's term, the world's attention was seized by a dramatic event far from the United States—the fall of Khartoum in Sudan on January 26, 1885, to the Muslim forces of Muhammad

Ahmad, the self-proclaimed Mahdi, the "Expected One" of Islam. The massacre of British general Charles Gordon, his entire Egyptian garrison, and thousands of civilians aroused horror and rage in Britain—sentiments shared in the United States and other countries of the West. The British would regain control of Sudan under general, later field marshall, Herbert Kitchener, in a smashing victory on September 2, 1898, at Omdurman, just outside Khartoum.

Free Trade and Former Presidents

Arthur continued to occupy a middle ground between the protectionism favored by many Republicans and the free trade preferred by the Democrats. In March 1884, he had won Senate ratification of a treaty permitting the importation without tariffs of certain Mexican goods—especially tobacco and sugar—in return for Mexico's elimination of tariffs on certain U.S. goods.[2] But lacking a strong political base, he failed to get Senate action on reciprocal trade treaties with Spain and the Dominican Republic. When Arthur left office, no vote had been taken. Among those blocking action was James G. Blaine. Opposition came from business groups such as the National Association of Wool Manufactures and from the union leader Samuel Gompers. Although business and labor organizations were often opponents, they both sought to protect their constituencies from foreign competition. When Cleveland assumed the presidency, he withdrew the treaties.[3]

On February 3, Arthur called for Congress to place Ulysses Grant, now dying of throat cancer, on the army's retired list so that he could receive a pension, part of which could be inherited by his widow. Because General Grant had resigned, not retired, from the service after winning the presidency in 1868, he was not eligible for a pension. Congress acted on March 4, shortly before adjourning, and Arthur signed the bill in the closing hours of his term.[4] The measure was a blessing for Grant, who had been financially ruined by a number of bad investments. He labored heroically during his last weeks of life to complete his memoirs, which

Mark Twain had arranged to publish, securing a comfortable income for Grant's widow, Julia.

On December 6, 1884, work on the Washington Monument was completed. A few weeks later, on February 21, the eve of Washington's birthday, Arthur dedicated the 555-foot obelisk. This was a powerfully moving event for Americans in general and for Arthur in particular as his presidency neared its end. The crowd gathered for the event was in good spirits, applauding Arthur's praise of Washington and the remarks by other speakers. That evening, he hosted his last public reception as president, greeting about three thousand well-wishers.

A New President

President-elect Cleveland arrived in Washington by train from Albany on March 2 and lodged the next two nights at the Arlington Hotel. He declined Arthur's invitation to stay at the White House, appreciating the graciousness of the offer, but preferring to wait until he officially moved in as president. Cleveland did pay his respects to Arthur at the White House shortly after his arrival. The next day, Arthur reciprocated, visiting Cleveland at the Arlington Hotel.

Inauguration Day, March 4, was warm and clear, and the mood of the crowed, numbering between thirty and fifty thousand, was jovial. Cleveland joined Arthur at the White House for the short carriage ride to the Capitol. Riding with them were Chief Justice Morrison Waite and the renowned historian George Bancroft, who had founded the United States Naval Academy at Annapolis while serving as secretary of the navy in the Polk administration. After Cleveland delivered his inaugural address and took the oath of office, he and Arthur returned to the White House, where they reviewed a procession and Arthur hosted a luncheon for the new president. That night, Arthur and his cabinet joined Cleveland for the inaugural ball, where they greeted the friendly crowd for over an hour.[5]

In spite of the assassinations of Lincoln and Garfield within the past twenty years, presidential security was still light. America's leaders worried about losing touch with the public and appearing too "royal." The *New York Tribune* warned that Americans did not want the president to be "the slave of his office, the prisoner of forms and restrictions."[6] Arthur reflected this mindset. The assassination of William McKinley in 1901 led to increased protection, but presidents still chafed at appearing remote or monarchical.

Retirement and Death

After staying a few days longer in Washington with former secretary of state Frelinghuysen, Arthur returned to New York City and began what would be one of the shorter post-presidencies, lasting just over twenty-one months. Financially he was comfortable, needing no presidential pension. He held stock, cash, and several valuable pieces of real estate in New York City and Long Branch, New Jersey. In addition, he received a thousand dollars per month from his old law firm with an impressive suite of offices on the fourth floor of the Mutual Life Building, even though his declining health precluded his contributing much more than his name.[7]

At times over the next year, he felt better, but the malady always returned, stronger than before. He still made some public appearances, for example, at the funeral of Frelinghuysen, who died of hepatitis on May 20, and at his son Alan's graduation from Princeton.

In February 1886, the disease worsened, the concomitant heart trouble furthering his decline. His two children and two of his sisters came to care for him. A transient rally in June led to his leaving the heat of New York to stay at a cottage in New London, Connecticut. The inevitable return of the malady left him weaker than ever. After his return to New York on October 1, Arthur was either bedridden or in a reclining chair for his last month. The few visitors he received included Chief Justice Waite and Rutherford Hayes, his harsh view of Arthur now modified. During these last days, he continued to reassure family and friends that he would improve; he made no appeals for sympathy. His doctor later lauded him, saying of Arthur that "he was a brave, strong man to the last, and few men deserved better to live."[8]

On November 16, two days before he died, Arthur felt better, dictated several letters, signed some legal documents, saw a few people, and ordered the destruction of most of his personal and official papers. He called in an old friend from Customhouse days, Jimmy Smith, to carry out the task. Arthur's son, Alan, stated that three large garbage cans were filled several times with these papers and everything burned.[9] The reasons for this action are not known; readers can only speculate. It is known that Arthur had come to regret some things he had done in his pre-presidential days. Perhaps the desire to expunge evidence of past malfeasance motivated him. Perhaps his predilection for privacy lay behind the decision. One can speculate, but no definite answer has been uncovered.

On the morning of November 17, Arthur was found unconscious from a massive cerebral hemorrhage. He died the following morning at five o'clock.

Later that day, Grover Cleveland issued an official proclamation in which he stated that Arthur's "assumption of the grave duties was marked by an evident and conscientious sense of his responsibilities, and earnest desire to meet them in a patriotic and benevolent spirit."[10]

This was a sincere expression from a man not given to official, *pro forma* kind words.

On Monday, November 22, a funeral service was held at the Episcopal Church of the Heavenly Rest, where his wife's service had been just under seven years before. Among the pallbearers were Walter Gresham, Robert Lincoln, William Chandler, Benjamin Brewster, Philip Sheridan, Charles Tiffany, and Cornelius Vanderbilt. President Cleveland and former President Hayes were there, along with Chief Justice Waite, justices Blatchford and Harlan, members of Congress, and diplomats. The mourners also included James G. Blaine and Roscoe Conkling, who would be dead himself in little more than a year.[11] Arthur's body was taken north and buried beside that of his wife in Albany Rural Cemetery.

Robert Lincoln summed up Arthur and his performance as president well:

> My acquaintance with him really began with my official connection. Not only did I learn to respect him most highly, but to have a great personal affection for him. It always seemed to me that he overcame in an admirable manner the difficulties surrounding him when he became President. While an earnest Republican, he was above all a patriotic citizen, and I know of no act in which he did not have at heart the public interest. I think it is universally conceded that, as far as he was actually responsible, he was able and dignified.... He was a President of whom the country is proud and for whom it may well mourn.[12]

This eulogy did not detail, but did recognize Arthur's health problems and his being caught between two factions of the Republican Party.

Memorials

In Fairfield, Vermont, Arthur's childhood home was reconstructed in 1953. The house and a granite monument dedicated in 1903 are part of the President Chester A. Arthur State Historical Site.[13] But there is no Arthur presidential center, no Arthur presidential library. A bronze plaque marks Arthur's former home, a five-story brownstone on Lexington Avenue in New York City, but nothing of his remains there and it is closed to the public. A few blocks away in Madison Square, a bronze statue close to eighteen feet tall was unveiled in 1899. Speaking at the ceremony was Elihu Root (1845–1937), who had known Arthur while practicing law in New York City and while serving as United States attorney for the Southern District of New York. Root was later secretary of war under McKinley and Theodore Roosevelt and then was appointed secretary of state by Roosevelt. In 1909, he was elected to the United

States Senate and was awarded the Nobel Peace Prize in 1912. At the unveiling, Root said of Arthur:

> He was wise in statesmanship and firm and effective in administration. Honesty in national finance, purity and effectiveness in the civil service, the promotion of commerce, the re-creation of the American navy, reconciliation between North and South and honorable friendship with foreign nations received his active support. Good causes found in him a friend and bad measures met in him an unyielding opponent.[14]

CHAPTER 17

Evaluation

I n *The American Republic* (1865), a work comparable in its subject and depth of insight to Tocqueville's *Democracy in America*, the political philosopher Orestes Brownson wrote that nations have purposes given them by God. He believed that the American mission is to secure:

> the authority of the public and the freedom of the individual—the sovereignty of the people without social despotism, and individual freedom without anarchy.... The Greek and Roman republics asserted the state to the detriment of individual freedom; modern republics either do the same, or assert individual freedom to the detriment of the state. The American republic has been instituted by Providence to realize the freedom of each with advantage to the other.[1]

Arthur passed on to Grover Cleveland a country in which these principles were alive and well. So looking back on Arthur's presidency, what accomplishments warrant the contention that he generally has been underrated?

Arthur seems to have shortchanged himself, for one thing, by following a career path that, though it brought him financial prosperity and social status, was not the *cursus honorum* by which his contemporaries Rutherford Hayes, James Garfield, Benjamin Harrison, Grover Cleveland, and William McKinley rose to the White House. Prior to serving as president, all had been elected to local office, all had been in Congress, and Hayes, Cleveland, and McKinley had been governors. Arthur's intelligence, knowledge, and stamina were comparable to these men's, but he did not reach for higher office until 1880. The reasons are not clear. Any written records he might have made of his thoughts and motives were burned as he lay dying. Perhaps, having been raised in modest economic circumstances, he wanted a sense of economic security.

Unlike Lincoln, Arthur faced no major crises that would have given him the opportunity to distinguish himself. He lacked the colorful and dominating personality of Andrew Jackson or Theodore Roosevelt, though there are hints that colorful and dominating traits were there to be developed had his health not declined. Yet in spite of his poor health, he effectively and efficiently handled the problems that confronted the United States during these relatively quiet years and left behind a country in better shape than when he came into office. The historian Samuel Eliot Morison asserted that "Arthur's administration stands up as the best Republican one between Lincoln and Theodore Roosevelt,"[2] an evaluation that places Arthur above Johnson, Grant, Hayes, Harrison, and McKinley.

After Arthur succeeded Garfield, the United States was without a vice president for almost three and a half years, but the source of Arthur's greatest anxiety was the period between July 2, 1881, when Garfield was shot, and his death on September 19, when the president was incapacitated but Arthur could not act as president. He called for Congress to clarify the circumstances under which the Constitution authorized the vice president to step in and serve:

It is provided by the second article of the Constitution, in the fifth clause of its first section, that "in case of the removal of the President from office, or of his death, resignation or inability to discharge the powers and duties of the said office, the same shall devolve on the Vice President."

What is the intendment of the Constitution in its specification of "inability to discharge the powers and duties of the said office" as one of the contingencies which calls the Vice-President to the exercise of Presidential functions?[3]

Vice President Arthur went on to ask what constituted an "inability to discharge the powers and duties of said office" and whether the president had any say in the matter. If the inability were temporary, what then?[4]

Congress would not address these potentially explosive questions for another eighty years. In 1967, after the deaths in office of William McKinley, Warren Harding, Franklin Delano Roosevelt, and John F. Kennedy and the long-term incapacitation of Woodrow Wilson, the Twenty-fifth Amendment to the Constitution was ratified, providing for the continuation of executive leadership if the president "is unable to discharge the powers and duties of his office." Balancing the need for uninterrupted executive authority against the danger of inviting a coup d'état, the amendment established procedures for the president to resume his duties as well as for a formal declaration of his incapacity.

The case can be made that the 1880s were the most productive decade in American history.[5] There were impressive gains in gross national product, business formation, manufacturing, and agricultural productivity. Real income for both industrial and agricultural workers rose. Arthur does not deserve all the credit, of course, but this astonishing progress did get underway during his presidency.

One of Arthur's most important achievements was the revival of the United States Navy, a key factor in our becoming a world power. The navy, which had been in decline since the end of the Civil War, benefitted from Arthur's leadership in overcoming resistance from shortsighted opponents who recognized no dangers, opposed spending money, or simply did not want to face America's vulnerability as a wealthy country with weak armed forces. The United States was starting to recognize not only that protecting order, justice, and freedom beyond its borders was the right thing to do, but also that it was beneficial to have friends rather than enemies in as much of the world as possible. History is clear about the short lifespans of large, wealthy, free countries with weak armed forces.

As the 1880s opened, much, perhaps most, of public sentiment opposed overseas expansion of American power. There were, though, those who realized that the United States was too big and too rich to remain free and prosperous while standing meekly on the sidelines while other countries expanded their empires. In the spring of 1880, John A. Kasson, the American minister to the Austro-Hungarian Empire, called for the reassertion of the Monroe Doctrine, backed up by a stronger navy, and the annexation of the still free Pacific islands, which would strengthen American trade and projection of power.[6] The *New York Tribune* agreed heartily with that policy, editorializing on June 6, 1881, that United States must keep the Danish West Indies (Virgin Islands) out of the hands of any European major power and stop the French from seizing Panama. These moves would strengthen American trade and put "the United States in the front rank of the great directing forces of human freedom and progress."[7]

Opposing this policy was the *New York Herald*, which on December 19, 1881, opined, "We have no outlying empires to protect; we have no vast standing army to employ; we have no navy to guard our coasts, because they can take care of themselves.... Our foreign policy is a domestic policy."[8]

This opposition to expansion and assertion of overseas power was the stronger of the two forces during the Arthur years. Still his administration did lay the foundations in foreign policy and naval might for the projection of American power by future presidents.

In just over thirteen years, the war with Spain would test the Arthur administration's reforms. The navy, by then one of the largest and most effective in the world, had some teething problems but performed well overall—especially in the Manila Bay engagement and in the clash just off Santiago, Cuba. Although the army, in contrast to the navy, did not grow dramatically during the Arthur years, it became better organized, and the quality of the small regular force improved. The war with Spain did cause it more problems than those encountered by the navy. The rapid expansion and the mounting of large expeditionary forces for operations in Cuba, Puerto Rico, and the Philippines severely strained the army, but it learned, and the war ended with American military capabilities substantially improved.

Arthur, too, was a determined backer of civil service reform. For years, proponents of "clean" government had talked of change, which finally began with the Pendleton Act. Arthur, however, did not have a powerful political movement, caught as he was between reformers who did not trust the sincerity of his conversion to good government and his former friends and colleagues in the Stalwart camp who saw him as a turncoat. His opposition to government pork was widely appreciated, even though he lost this battle to those in Congress who opposed reform. In addition, Arthur espoused lower tariffs, but here, too, he could not overcome the opposition of congressional opponents of even modest reform. He was a brave man with sound principles, but his weak political base precluded his accomplishing more during his presidency.

The 1880s was a decade of calm progress, growing prosperity, and spreading opportunities for women and ethnic minorities. There were, however, those who were impatient with the pace, who wanted change more rapidly and radically. As the decade closed, these new forces—espousing, for example, socialism and religious systems rejecting biblical beliefs—challenged the established culture, which was based on the Christian faith and individual initiative. Some change, such as the expanding freedom for women and ethnic minorities, was good. But attacking the foundations of the country were those wanting to extirpate Christian culture, not just give opportunity to those who differ from it. Calls were heard also from a few radical voices wanting to substitute economic collectivism for economic freedom. These disruptions would accelerate during the 1880s, although the foundational principles withstood them and remain to this day, still threatened but undaunted. Often challenges to belief systems force people to reevaluate these principles, appreciate them better, and strengthen societal foundations. This we Americans have experienced. Arthur was a key man among those who stood firmly for the maintenance and strengthening of these foundational beliefs.

All things considered, Arthur deserves to be reexamined and remembered with respect and appreciation for his role in pulling the country together after the Garfield assassination in spite of severe, even terminal, health problems and strong opposition within his own party. In March 1885 he turned over to Grover Cleveland a country which had rebounded well from the dark summer of 1881.

Notes

Chapter 1: The Unexpected

1. Kenneth D. Ackerman, *Dark Horse: The Surprise Election and Political Murder of President James A. Garfield* (New York: Carroll and Graf Publishers, 2003), 372–79.
2. Candice Millard, *Destiny of the Republic: A Tale of Madness, Medicine, and the Murder of a President* (New York: Doubleday, 2011), 231–32.

Chapter 2: Early Years

1. George Frederick Howe, *Chester A. Arthur: A Quarter-Century of Machine Politics* (New York: Frederick Ungar Publishing Co., 1935), 8–9.
2. Rita Stevens, *Chester A. Arthur: 21st President of the United States* (Ada, Oklahoma: Garrett Educational Corporation, 1989), 12.
3. James Humes, *Which President Killed a Man: Tantalizing Trivia and Fun Facts about Chief Executives and First Ladies* (New York: MJF Books), 40.
4. Gerard W. Gawalt, *My Dear President: Letters Between Presidents and their Wives* (New York: Black Dog and Leventhal Publishers, 2005), 57–60.
5. "William Lewis Herndon," Wikipedia, https://en.wikipedia.org/wiki/William_Lewis_Herndon.

Chapter 3: Political Rise

1. Paul F. Boller Jr., *Presidential Campaigns* (New York: Oxford University Press, 1984), 113.
2. David C. Whitney and Robin Vaughn Whitney, *The American Presidents* (Pleasantville, New York: The Reader's Digest Association, 2001), 521.
3. Geoffrey Perret, *Lincoln's War: The Untold Story of America's Greatest President as Commander in Chief* (New York: Random House, 2004), 300–304.
4. Thomas C. Reeves, *Gentleman Boss: The Life and Times of Chester Arthur* (New York: Alfred A. Knopf, 1975), 30.
5. Ibid.
6. Ibid., 33.
7. Ibid., 42–44.

Chapter 4: Machine Politician

1. George Frederick Howe, *Chester A. Arthur: A Quarter-Century of Machine Politics* (New York: Frederick Ungar Publishing Co., 1935), 48–49.
2. Thomas C. Reeves, *Gentleman Boss: The Life and Times of Chester Arthur* (New York: Alfred A. Knopf, 1975), 62–63, 68.
3. Jean Edward Smith, *Grant* (New York: Simon and Schuster, 2001), 548.
4. Ibid., 548–49.
5. Joseph Nathan Kane, *Facts about the Presidents* (New York: Ace Books, 1976), 113.
6. Ibid.
7. Page Smith, *The Rise of Industrial America*, Vol. 6 of *A People's History of the Post-Reconstruction Era* (New York: McGraw-Hill Book Company, 1984), 231.
8. Frederick Douglass, *Selected Speeches and Writings*, ed. Philip S. Foner (Chicago: Lawrence Hill Books, 1999), 598–600.
9. Lois Beachy Underhill, *The Woman Who Ran for President: The Many Lives of Victoria Woodhull* (Bridgehampton, N.Y.: Bridge Works Publishing Co., 1995), 208.

10. Ibid., 211–12.
11. Ibid., 217–18.
12. Paul F. Boller Jr., *Presidential Inaugurations* (San Diego, California: Harcourt, 2001), 129.
13. Smith, *Grant*, 596.
14. William A. DeGregorio, *The Complete Book of U.S. Presidents* (Fort Lee, New Jersey: Barricade Books, 1993), 285.
15. Ibid.

Chapter 5: Clash with Hayes

1. Thomas C. Reeves, *Gentleman Boss: The Life and Times of Chester Arthur* (New York: Alfred A. Knopf, 1975), 113.
2. John Sherman, *John Sherman's Recollections of Forty Years in the House, Senate and Cabinet: An Autobiography*, Vol. II (New York: Greenwood Press, 1968), 676.
3. Hans L. Trefousse, *Rutherford B. Hayes* (New York: Times Books, 2002), 93, 95, 101.
4. Ibid., 107.
5. Reeves, *Gentleman Boss*, 158, 276.

Chapter 6: Up to Second Place

1. Jean Edward Smith, *Grant* (New York: Simon and Schuster, 2001), 616–17.
2. Ibid., 617.
3. Ibid., 616.
4. Thomas C. Reeves, *Gentleman Boss: The Life and Times of Chester Arthur* (New York: Alfred A. Knopf, 1975), 180.
5. Kenneth D. Ackerman, *Dark Horse: The Surprise Election and Political Murder of President James A. Garfield* (New York: Carroll and Graf Publishers, 2003), 161.
6. Paul F. Boller Jr., *Presidential Inaugurations* (San Diego, California: Harcourt, 2001), 144.
7. Theodore Clarke Smith, *The Life and Letters of James Abram Garfield: 1877–1882*, Vol. 2 (No city: Archon Books, 1968), 670.
8. Ackerman, *Dark Horse*, 231, 234, 240.

9. Ibid., 242–44.

10. George Frederick Howe, *Chester A. Arthur: A Quarter-Century of Machine Politics* (New York: Frederick Ungar Publishing Co., 1935), 129–30.

11. Jules Witcover, *The American Vice Presidency: From Irrelevance to Power* (Washington, D.C.: Smithsonian Books, 2014), 191.

12. Ibid., 134.

13. Smith, *The Life and Letters of James Abram Garfield*, 1119.

14. Ibid., 1129.

15. Zachary Karabell, *Chester Alan Arthur* (New York: Times Books, 2004), 57.

16. Rutherford Birchard Hayes, *Diary and Letters of Rutherford Birchard Hayes: 1881–1893*, Vol. IV, ed. Charles Richard Williams (Columbus, Ohio: the Ohio State Archaeological and Historical Society, 1925), 23.

17. Ibid., 151.

18. Thomas J. Whalen, *A Higher Purpose: Profiles in Presidential Courage* (Chicago: Ivan R. Dee, 2007), 53.

19. Howe, *Chester A. Arthur*, 155.

Chapter 7: The New President

1. James D. Richardson, ed., *A Compilation of the Messages and Papers of the Presidents*, Vol. XI (New York: Bureau of National Literature, 1897), 4620.

2. Ibid., 4621.

3. Until the end of the nineteenth century, the title "ambassador" was used only by the great powers of Europe—Britain, France, Germany, Austria-Hungary, and Russia. The United States raised its ministers to the rank of ambassador in 1893.

4. Zachary Karabell, *Chester Alan Arthur*, (New York: Times Books, 2004), 71.

5. Kenneth D. Ackerman, *Dark Horse: The Surprise Election and Political Murder of President James A. Garfield* (New York: Carroll and Graf Publishers, 2003), 436.

6. Ibid., 437.

7. Peter Charles Hoffer, Williamjames Hull Hoffer, and N. E. H. Hull, *The Supreme Court: An Essential History* (Lawrence, Kansas: University Press of Kansas, 2007), 136.
8. Ibid.
9. John Whitcomb and Claire Whitcomb, *Real Life at the White House: Two Hundred Years of Daily Life at America's Most Famous Residence* (New York: Routledge, 2000), 183.
10. Thomas C. Reeves, *Gentleman Boss: The Life and Times of Chester Arthur* (New York: Alfred A. Knopf, 1975), 268–69.
11. Ibid., 270-71.
12. Justus D. Doenecke, *The Presidencies of James A. Garfield and Chester A. Arthur* (Lawrence: University Press of Kansas, 1981), 79.
13. Lynn Sherr, *Failure Is Impossible: Susan B. Anthony in Her Own Words* (New York: Times Books, 1995), 267–68.
14. Perry M. Rogers, ed. *Aspects of Western Civilization: Problems and Sources in History*, Vol. II (Upper Saddle River, New Jersey: Prentice Hall, 1988), 254–55.
15. Lois W. Banner, *Elizabeth Cady Stanton: A Radical for Women's Rights* (Boston: Little, Brown and Company, 1980), 76.
16. Julie Husband and Jim O'Loughlin, *Daily Life in the Industrial United States, 1870–1900* (Westport, Connecticut: Greenwood Press, 2004), 212.
17. David Colbert, *Eye Witness to Wall Street: Four Hundred Years of Dreamers, Schemers, Busts and Booms* (New York: Broadway Books, 2001), 68–70.
18. Brooke Kroeger, *Nellie Bly: Daredevil, Reporter, Feminist* (New York: Times Books, 1994), 5, 21, 41.
19. Ibid., 172.
20. James D. Richardson, ed., *A Compilation of the Messages and Papers of the Presidents*, Vol. XI (New York: Bureau of National Literature, 1909), 4644.
21. Ibid.
22. Ibid.
23. Andrew C. Isenberg, *Wyatt Earp: A Vigilante Life* (New York: Hill and Wang, 2013), 152–55, 217; William Weir, *Written with*

Lead: America's Most Famous and Notorious Gunfights from the Revolutionary War to Today (New York: Cooper Square Press, 2003), 118–21.

24. Casey Tefertiller, *Wyatt Earp: The Life Behind the Legend* (New York: John Wiley and Sons, 1997), 252–53.

25. Maurice Matloff, ed., *American Military History Volume 1: 1775–1902* (Conshohocken, Pennsylvania: Combined Books, 1996), 282.

Chapter 8: Arthur and Race

1. John Keegan, *Fields of Battle: The Wars for North America* (New York: Alfred A. Knopf, 1996), 311.

2. Robert M. Utley and Wilcomb E. Washburn, *Indian Wars* (Boston: Houghton Mifflin Company, 2002), 281.

3. Paul Andrew Hutton, *The Apache Wars: The Hunt for Geronimo, the Apache Kid, and the Captive Boy Who Started the Longest War in American History* (New York: Crown, 2016), 386–87.

4. James D. Richardson, ed. *A Compilation of the Messages and Papers of the Presidents, Vol. XI* (New York: Bureau of National Literature, 1897), 4642.

5. Ibid.

6. Larry Schweikart, Dave Dougherty, and Michael Allen, *Essential Documents for Every American* (New York: Sentinel 2011), 203.

7. Bill Neeley, *The Last Comanche Chief: The Life and Times of Quanah Parker* (New York: John Wiley and Sons, 1995), 32.

8. Ibid., 45–47, 52, 54. Cynthia Parker's birth and death dates are uncertain, there being no official records of either date. From the evidence that exists, it seems likely that she died in 1871, in her mid-forties, but she might have died as early as 1864.

9. Ibid., 174, 179, 199.

10. Ibid., 168, 222–23, 229.

11. Ibid., 151.

12. David Hackett Fischer, *Liberty and Freedom* (New York: Oxford University Press, 2015), 387–88.

13. John A. Garraty and Mark C. Carnes, eds. *American National Biography*, Vol. 11 (New York: Oxford University Press, 1999), 747–48.
14. Julian E. Zelizer, ed., *The American Congress: The Building of Democracy* (Boston: Houghton Mifflin Company, 2004), 255.
15. Ibid., 256.
16. Gail Buckley, *American Patriots: The Story of Blacks in the Military from the Revolution to Desert Storm* (New York: Random House, 2001), 131.
17. Thomas Sowell, *Education: Assumptions Versus History* (Stanford, California: Hoover Institution Press, 1986), 30.
18. Ibid.
19. Garraty and Carnes, eds. *American National Biography*, Vol. 22, 507–508.
20. Gail Buckley, *American Patriots: The Story of Blacks in the Military from the Revolution to Desert Storm* (New York: Random House, 2001), 125.
21. Ibid., 127–28.
22. Garraty and Carnes, eds., *American National Biography*, Vol. 23, 316–17.
23. Ibid.
24. Frederick Douglass, *Selected Speeches and Writings*, Philip S. Foner, ed. (Chicago: Lawrence Hill Books, 1999), 656–57.
25. Ibid., 667.
26. Robert J. Norrell, *Up From History: The Life of Booker T. Washington* (Cambridge, Massachusetts: the Belknap Press of Harvard University, 2009), 30–35, 39.
27. Ibid., 40.
28. David Levering Lewis, *W. E. B. Du Bois, 1919–1963: The Fight for Equality and the American Century* (New York: Henry Holt and Company, 2000), 571.
29. Frederick Douglass, *Life and Times of Frederick Douglass: Written by Himself* (New York: Collier Books, Macmillan Publishing Company, 1962), 536–37.

Chapter 9: Taking Charge

1. Ari Hoogenboom, *Outlawing the Spoils: A History of the Civil Service Reform Movement, 1865–1883* (Urbana: University of Illinois Press, 1961), 213.
2. Ibid., 215–16.
3. John M. Pafford, *The Forgotten Conservative: Rediscovering Grover Cleveland* (Washington, D.C.: Regnery History, 2013), 11–12.
4. Hoogenboom, *Outlawing the Spoils*, 236–37.
5. Paul P. Van Riper, *History of the United States Civil Service* (Evanston, Illinois: Row, Peterson and Company, 1958), 103.
6. Ibid., 105.
7. Ibid., 130.
8. Hoogenboom, *Outlawing the Spoils*, 264.
9. Richard Slotkin, *The Long Road to Antietam: How the Civil War Became a Revolution* (New York: Liveright, 2012), 58–59.
10. Herman Hathaway, *Shades of Blue and Gray: An Introductory Military History of the Civil War* (Columbia: University of Missouri Press), 93–94; Geoffrey Perett, *Lincoln's War: The Untold Story of America's Greatest President as Commander in Chief* (New York: Random House, 2004), 209.
11. David Herbert Donald, *Lincoln* (New York: Simon and Schuster, 1995), 385.
12. James D. Richardson, ed. *A Compilation of the Messages and Papers of the Presidents, Vol. XI* (New York: Bureau of National Literature, 1897), 4712.
13. Eleanor Berman, *Eyewitness Travel: New York City* (New York: DK Publishing, 2011), 86–87.
14. David McCullough, *The Great Bridge* (New York: Touchstone, 1972), 521.
15. Thomas C. Reeves, *Gentleman Boss: The Life and Times of Chester Arthur* (New York: Alfred A. Knopf, 1975), 359–60.
16. McCullough, *The Great Bridge*, 532.
17. Reeves, *Gentleman Boss*, 360.

Chapter 10: Conflicts Intensify

1. Joyce Appleby, *The Relentless Revolution: A History of Capitalism* (New York: Norton, 2010), 218.
2. Julie Husband and Jim O'Loughlin, *Daily Life in the Industrial United States, 1870–1900* (Westport, Connecticut: Greenwood Press, 2004), 238.
3. Leonard Dinnerstein and David Reimers, *Ethnic Americans: A History of Immigration* (New York: Columbia University Press, 1999), 18.
4. Thomas Sowell, *Migration and Cultures: A World View* (New York: Basic Books, 1996), 221–24.
5. Sean Dennis Cashman, *America in the Gilded Age: From the Death of Lincoln to the Rise of Theodore Roosevelt* (New York: New York University Press, 1984), 89.
6. Ibid.
7. Thomas C. Reeves, *Gentleman Boss: The Life of Chester Alan Arthur* (Newtown, Connecticut: American Political Biography Press, 1991), 278.
8. James D. Richardson, ed., *A Compilation of the Messages and Papers of the Presidents*, Vol. XI (New York: Bureau of National Literature, Inc., 1897), 4699.
9. Richardson, ed. *A Compilation of the Messages and Papers of the Presidents*, Vol. X, 4708.
10. H. Wayne Morgan, *From Hayes to McKinley: National Party Politics 1877–1896* (Syracuse, N.Y.: Syracuse University Press, 1969), 158.
11. John M. Pafford, *The Forgotten Conservative: Rediscovering Grover Cleveland* (Washington, D.C.: Regnery History, 2013), 55.
12. Thomas Sowell, *Basic Economics: A Common Sense Guide to the Economy* (New York: Basic Books, 2007), 345–46.
13. James Rickards, *The Death of Money: The Coming Collapse of the International Monetary System* (New York: Penguin, 2014), 234.
14. Ron Paul and Lewis Lehrman, *The Case For Gold: A Minority Report of the U.S. Gold Commission* (Washington: Cato Institute, 1982), 97–98.

15. Ibid., 102.
16. Ibid., 109–10.
17. Ibid., 120.
18. Ibid., 167.
19. Richardson, ed., *A Compilation of the Messages and Papers of the Presidents*, Vol. XI, 4830.
20. Reeves, *Gentleman Boss*, 216.
21. Ibid., 301.
22. Ibid., 302.
23. Ibid., 304.
24. Simon Winchester, *Krakatoa: The Day the World Exploded: August 27, 1883* (New York: HarperCollins, 2003), 132, 136, 154–55.
25. Ibid.
26. Lewis E. Lloyd, *Tariffs: The Case For Protection* (New York: Devin-Adair, 1955), 14–17.
27. Tom E. Terrill, *The Tariff, Politics, and American Foreign Policy 1874–1901* (Westport, Connecticut: Greenwood Press, 1973), 17.
28. Clarence A. Wiley, *Economics and Politics of the Agricultural Tariff* (New York: H. W. Wilson, 1927), 40.
29. Terrill, *The Tariff, Politics, and American Foreign Policy, 1874–1901*, 17.
30. Ibid., 18.
31. Ibid.
32. Ibid., 52–53.
33. Ibid., 80–81, 70.

Chapter 11: Reforming the Armed Forces

1. Max Boot, *The Savage Wars of Peace: Small Wars and the Rise of American Power* (New York: Basic Books, 2002), 57.
2. Samuel Eliot Morison, *The Oxford History of the American People* (New York: Oxford University Press, 1965), 748.
3. Robert W. Love Jr., *History of the U.S. Navy, Vol. I, 1775–1941* (Harrisburg, Pennsylvania., 1992), 331.
4. George Dewey, *Autobiography of George Dewey* (New York: AMS Press, 1969), 150, 154.

5. Boot, *The Savage Wars of Peace*, 62.
6. Paul Kennedy, *The Rise and Fall of the Great Powers: Economic Change and Military Conflict from 1500–2000* (New York: Random House, 1987), 203.
7. Robley D. Evans, *A Sailor's Log* (New York: D. Appleton, 1901), 229–30.
8. Love, *History of the U.S. Navy, Vol. I*, 346, 350.
9. James D. Richardson, ed., *A Compilation of the Messages and Papers of the Presidents*, Vol. XI (New York: Bureau of National Literature, Inc., 1897), 4727–4728.
10. Ibid., 4727.
11. Rita Stevens, *Chester A. Arthur: 21st President of the United States* (Ada, Oklahoma: Garrett Educational Corporation, 1989), 101.
12. Kennedy, *The Rise and Fall of the Great Powers*, 226.
13. Love, *History of the U.S. Navy, Vol. I, 1775–1941*, 349–50.
14. Boot, *The Savage Wars of Peace*, 62.
15. Ibid., 351.
16. Ibid., 352–53.
17. Ibid.
18. Brayton Harris, *The Navy Times Book of Submarines: A Political, Social, and Military History* (New York: Berkley Books, 1997), 8–13, 32–33, 89–99.
19. Ibid., 105, 107.
20. Richard S. West Jr., *Admirals of American Empire: The Combined Story of George Dewey, Alfred Thayer Mahan, Winfield Scott Schley, and William Thomas Sampson* (Westport, Connecticut: Greenwood Press, 1971), 108–11.
21. Michael Goley and John S. Bowman, *North American Exploration* (Hoboken, New Jersey: John Wiley and Sons, 2013), 432–33.
22. Ibid., 433.
23. John A. Garraty and Mark C. Carnes, eds. *American National Biography*, Vol. 11 (New York: Oxford University Press, 1999), 94–95.

24. Albert Gleaves, *Life and Letters of Rear Admiral Stephen B. Luce* (New York: Putnam's, 1925), 168–69.
25. Ivan Musicant, *Empire by Default: The Spanish-American War and the Dawn of the American Century* (New York: Henry Holt and Company, 1998), 5–9.
26. West, *Admirals of American Empire*, 77, 120–123.
27. Kennedy, *The Rise and Fall of the Great Powers*, 201–3.
28. John S. Goff, *Robert Todd Lincoln: A Man in His Own Right* (Norman: University of Oklahoma Press, 1969), 127.
29. Musicant, *Empire by Default*, 250.
30. Goff, *Robert Todd Lincoln*, 60–65.
31. Stanley P. Hirshson, *The White Tecumseh: A Biography of General William T. Sherman* (New York: Wiley, 1997), 375.
32. Musicant, *Empire by Default*, 250, 270.
33. Ibid., 270.
34. Roy Morris Jr., *Sheridan: The Life and Wars of General Phil Sheridan* (New York: Crown, 1992), 380.
35. Goff, *Robert Todd Lincoln: A Man in His Own Right*, 131.

Chapter 12: Central American Canal

1. Ivan Musicant, *The Banana Wars: A History of United States Military Intervention in Latin America from the Spanish-American War to the Invasion of Panama* (New York: Macmillan, 1990), 83.
2. Ibid.
3. Ibid., 83–84.
4. Geoffrey Perret, *Ulysses S. Grant: Soldier and President* (New York: Random House, 1997), 393.
5. Harry Barnard, *Rutherford B. Hayes and His America* (Indianapolis, Indiana: Bobbs Merrill, 1954), 442.
6. James D. Richardson, ed., *A Compilation of the Messages and Papers of the Presidents*, Vol. XI (New York: Bureau of National Literature, Inc., 1897), 4846.
7. Ibid., 4844.
8. Ibid., 4845.
9. Ibid.

10. David M. Pletcher, *The Awkward Years: American Foreign Relations under Garfield and Arthur* (Columbia: University of Missouri Press, 1962), 112.
11. George Frederick Howe, *Chester A. Arthur: A Quarter-Century of Machine Politics* (New York: Frederick Ungar Publishing Co., 1935), 274–75.

Chapter 13: Foreign Policy

1. William Benton, *The Annals of America, Vol. 10, 1868–1883: Reconstruction and Industrialization* (Chicago: Encyclopedia Britannica, 1976), 509.
2. David M. Pletcher, *The Awkward Years: American Foreign Relations under Garfield and Arthur* (Columbia: University of Missouri Press, 1962), 244.
3. Michael C. Meyer and William H. Beezley, eds., *The Oxford History of Mexico* (New York: Oxford University Press, 2000), 397–414.
4. Walter La Feber, *The Cambridge History of American Foreign Relations, Vol. II, The American Search for Opportunity, 1865–1913* (New York: Cambridge University Press, 1993), 84–86.
5. Ibid., 85–86.
6. Thomas Pakenham, *The Scramble for Africa: 1876–1912* (New York: Random House, 1991), 244, 246.
7. Ibid., 86.
8. Thomas C. Reeves, *Gentleman Boss: The Life and Times of Chester Arthur* (New York: Alfred A. Knopf, 1975), 403.
9. Julia Flynn Siler, *Lost Kingdom: Hawaii's Last Queen, the Sugar Kings, and America's First Imperial Adventure* (New York: Atlantic Monthly Press, 2012), 90.
10. Ibid., 149.
11. Pletcher, *The Awkward Years*, 70.
12. Robert W. Love Jr., *History of the U.S. Navy, Vol. I, 1775–1941* (Harrisburg, Pennsylvania., 1992), 359.
13. John M. Pafford, *The Forgotten Conservative: Rediscovering Grover Cleveland* (Washington, D.C.: Regnery History, 2013), 61.
14. Pletcher, *The Awkward Years*, 127–28.

15. Tom E. Terrill, *The Tariff, Politics, and American Foreign Policy 1874–1901* (Westport, Conn.: Greenwich Press, 1973), 19.
16. Pletcher, *The Awkward Years*, 206–8.
17. Ibid., 211.
18. Michael B. Oren, *Power, Faith, and Fantasy: America in the Middle East, 1776 to the Present* (New York: Norton, 2007), 291.
19. Ibid.

Chapter 14: Society

1. Rod Dreher, *The Benedict Option: A Strategy for Christians in a Post-Christian Nation* (New York: Sentinel, 2017), 39.
2. Ron Chernow, *Titan: The Life of John D. Rockefeller Sr.* (New York: Vintage, 1998), 191.
3. Clarence B. Carson, *A Basic History of the United States, Vol. IV, The Growth of America 1878–1928* (Wadley, Alabama: American Textbook Committee, 1985), 13.
4. F. E. Mayer, *The Religious Bodies of America* (St. Louis: Concordia, 1961), 335–36.
5. John A. Garraty and Mark C. Carnes, eds. *American National Biography, Vol. 5* (New York: Oxford University Press, 1999), 780.
6. Edith L. Blumhofer, *Her Heart Can See: The Life and Hymns of Fanny J. Crosby* (Grand Rapids, Michigan: Eerdmans, 2005), 220.
7. Thomas Bokenkotter, *A Concise History of the Catholic Church* (New York: Doubleday, 1966), 370.
8. Mark A. Noll, *A History of Christianity in the United States and Canada* (Grand Rapids, Mich.: Eerdmans, 1992), 348.
9. Julie Husband and Jim O'Loughlin, *Daily Life in the Industrial United States, 1870–1900* (Westport, Connecticut: Greenwood Press, 2004), 224.
10. Ibid., 229.
11. Patrick W. Carey, *Catholics in America: A History* (Westport, Connecticut, Praeger, 2004), 49.
12. Noll, *A History of Christianity in the United States and Canada*, 356.

13. Gerard F. Yates, ed., *Papal Thought on the State: Excerpts from Encyclicals and Other Writings of Recent Popes* (New York: Appleton-Century Crofts), 3.
14. Ibid., 13.
15. Ibid., 22.
16. Husband and O'Loughlin, *Daily Life in the Industrial United States 1870–1900*, 132, 135–36.
17. Ibid., 133.
18. Ibid., 133–34.
19. John McManners, ed., *The Oxford Illustrated History of Christianity* (Oxford: Oxford University Press, 1990), 40.
20. Douglas Southall Freeman, *Patriot and President, Vol. Six of George Washington: A Biography* (New York: Charles Scribner's Sons, 1954), 275–76.
21. Jonathan D. Sarna, *American Judaism: A History* (New Haven, Connecticut: Yale University Press, 2004), 63.
22. Husband and O'Loughlin, *Daily Life in the Industrial United States 1870–1900*, 136.
23. Garraty and Carnes, eds., *American National Biography, Vol. 8*, 33–34.
24. Noll, *A History of Christianity in the United States and Canada*, 371.
25. Ibid.
26. Garraty and Carnes, eds., *American National Biography, Vol. 21*, 147–48.
27. Robert Maynard Hutchins, ed., *Great Books of the Western World, Vol. 50, Marx* (Chicago: Encyclopaedia Britannica, 1952), 419.
28. Ibid.
29. Ibid., 434.
30. Philip Hamburger, *Separation of Church and State* (Cambridge, Massachusetts: Harvard University Press, 2002), 327–28.
31. Ibid., 314.
32. Ibid., 332.
33. Husband and O'Loughlin, *Daily Life in the Industrial United States 1870–1900*, 20.

34. Garraty and Carnes, eds., *American National Biography, Vol. 17,* 937.
35. Ibid., 938.
36. John M. Pafford, *The Forgotten Conservative: Rediscovering Grover Cleveland* (Washington, D.C.: Regnery History, 2013), 99–102.
37. Sean Dennis Cashman, *America in the Gilded Age: From the Death of Lincoln to the Rise of Theodore Roosevelt* (New York: New York University Press, 1984), 81, 83.
38. Husband and O'Loughlin, *Daily Life in the Industrial United States 1870–1900,* 159–60.
39. Julian E. Zelizer, ed., *The American Congress: The Building of Democracy* (Boston: Houghton Mifflin, 2004), 411–12.
40. Garraty and Carnes, eds., *American National Biography, Vol. 8,* 849–50.
41. Edmund Morris, *The Rise of Theodore Roosevelt* (New York: Random House, 2001), 356–57.
42. Lawrence Goldstone, *Drive: Henry Ford, George Selden, and the Race to Invent the Auto Age* (New York: Ballantine, 2016), 15–16.
43. Ibid., 27–28, 34.
44. L. Scott Bailey, editor-in-chief, *General Motors: The First 75 Years of Transportation Products* (Detroit: Automobile Quarterly Publications, 1983), 132–33.
45. Samuel Eliot Morison, *The Oxford History of the American People* (New York: Oxford University Press, 1965), 743–44.
46. Allan C. Bogue, *Frederick Jackson Turner: Strange Roads Going Down* (Norman: University of Oklahoma Press, 1998), 91, 97.
47. Joseph Wheelan, *Terrible Swift Sword: The Life of General Philip Sheridan* (Cambridge, Massachusetts: Da Capo Press, 2012), 302–4.
48. Cody's award was rescinded in 1916 on the grounds that he was a civilian, but it was restored posthumously by an Act of Congress in 1989.

49. Garraty and Carnes, *American National Biography, Vol. 5*, 134–35.
50. Jim Dwyer, project editor, *Strange Stories, Amazing Facts of America's Past* (Pleasantville, New York: Reader's Digest Association, 1989), 224.
51. David Nemec, *The Great Encyclopedia of Nineteenth-Century Major League Baseball* (Tuscaloosa, Alabama: University of Alabama Press, 2006), 156.
52. Ibid., 183.
53. Garraty and Carnes, eds. *American National Biography, Vol. 4*, 263–65.
54. Garraty and Carnes, eds. *American National Biography, Vol. 21*, 115–17.
55. David M. Fisher, *Lacrosse: A History of the Game* (Baltimore: Johns Hopkins University Press, 2002), 1–5.
56. Ibid., 5.
57. Irving Holodin, *The Story of the Metropolitan Opera 1883–1950: A Candid History* (New York: Alfred A. Knopf, 1953), 5, 89.
58. Morison, *The Oxford History of the American People*, 779.
59. Ibid.
60. James F. Cooper, *Knights of the Brush: The Hudson River School and the Moral Landscape* (New York: Hudson Hills Press, 2000), 19.
61. Garraty and Carnes, *American National Biography, Vol. 2*, 211–13.

Chapter 15: 1884 Election

1. Thomas C. Reeves, *Gentleman Boss: The Life and Times of Chester Arthur* (New York: Alfred A. Knopf, 1975), 371.
2. George Frederick Howe, *Chester A. Arthur: A Quarter-Century of Machine Politics* (New York: Frederick Ungar Publishing Co., 1935), 258.
3. Ibid., 258–59.
4. David M. Pletcher, *The Awkward Years: American Foreign Relations under Garfield and Arthur* (Columbia: University of Missouri Press, 1962), 258–59.

5. Lewis L. Gould, *Grand Old Party: A History of the Republicans* (Oxford: Oxford University Press, 2012), 63.
6. Ibid., 100.
7. Lee Kennett, *Sherman: A Soldier's Life* (New York: HarperCollins, 2001), 333.
8. Edmund Morris, *The Rise of Theodore Roosevelt* (New York: Random House, 2001), 252.
9. John S. Goff, *Robert Todd Lincoln: A Man in His Own Right* (Norman: University of Oklahoma Press, 1969), 142–43.
10. Ibid., 143.
11. Morris, *The Rise of Theodore Roosevelt*, 261.
12. Goff, *Robert Todd Lincoln*, 144.
13. Reeves, *Gentleman Boss*, 378–79.
14. H. Paul Jeffers, *An Honest President: The Life and Presidencies of Grover Cleveland* (New York: William Morrow, 2000), 96–97.
15. John M. Pafford, *The Forgotten Conservative: Rediscovering Grover Cleveland* (Washington, D.C.: Regnery History, 2013), 22.
16. Reeves, *Gentleman Boss*, 381.
17. Pafford, *The Forgotten Conservative*, 23–25.
18. Pletcher, *The Awkward Years*, 265–66.
19. Pafford, *The Forgotten Conservative*, 8–9.
20. Ibid., 27–28.
21. Pletcher, *The Awkward Years*, 264.
22. Pafford, *The Forgotten Conservative*, 29.
23. Ibid., 28–29.
24. Irving Stone, *They Also Ran: The Story of the Men Who Were Defeated for the Presidency* (Garden City, New York: Doubleday, Doran and Company, 1944), 248.
25. Richard White, *The Republic for Which It Stands: The United States during Reconstruction and the Gilded Age, 1865–1896* (New York: Oxford University Press, 2017), 472–74.
26. Reeves, *Gentleman Boss*, 387.
27. Howard Wayne Morgan, *From Hayes to McKinley: National Party Politics, 1877–1896,* (Syracuse, New York: Syracuse University Press, 1969), 233.

28. Ibid.

29. Russell Kirk, *The Roots of American Order* (Malibu, California: Pepperdine University Press, 1977), 467.

Chapter 16: The Last Act

1. Edwin Howard Simmons, *The United States Marines: A History* (Annapolis, Maryland: Naval Institute Press, 2003), 65.

2. George Frederick Howe, *Chester A. Arthur: A Quarter-Century of Machine Politics* (New York: Frederick Ungar Publishing Co., 1935), 286.

3. Ibid., 271.

4. Thomas C. Reeves, *Gentleman Boss: The Life and Times of Chester Arthur* (New York: Alfred A. Knopf, 1975), 414–15.

5. Ibid., 415–16.

6. Ronald Kessler, *The First Family Detail: Secret Service Agents Reveal the Hidden Lives of the Presidents* (New York: Crown Forum, 2014), 168.

7. Reeves, *Gentleman Boss*, 416.

8. Ibid., 417.

9. Ibid., 417–18.

10. H. Paul Jeffers, *An Honest President: Life and Presidencies of Grover Cleveland* (New York: William Morrow, 2000), 191.

11. Ibid., 418.

12. John S. Goff, *Robert Todd Lincoln: A Man in His Own Right* (Norman: University of Oklahoma Press, 1969), 152–53.

13. Peter Hannaford, *Presidential Retreats: Where They Went and Why They Went There* (New York: Threshold Editions, 2012), 114.

14. Reeves, *Gentleman Boss*, 419.

Chapter 17: Evaluation

1. Orestes A. Brownson, *The American Republic* (Wilmington, Delaware: ISI Books, 2003), 3.

2. Samuel Eliot Morison, *The Oxford History of the American People* (New York: Oxford University Press, 1965), 738.

3. James D. Richardson, ed., *A Compilation of the Messages and Papers of the Presidents*, *Vol. XI* (New York: Bureau of National Literature, 1897), 4652.
4. Ibid.
5. Ron Paul and Lewis Lehrman, *The Case for Gold* (Washington: Cato Institute, 1982), 106.
6. David M. Pletcher, *The Awkward Years: American Foreign Relations under Garfield and Arthur* (Columbia: University of Missouri Press, 1962), 10.
7. Ibid., 11.
8. Ibid.

Index

A

Adams, Charles Francis, 25–26, 164
Adams, Charles Francis Jr., 164
Adams, John Quincy, 6, 25, 31
American Federation of Labor, 88, 145
American Indians, 53, 62–71, 151
American Protestantism, 139
American Railway Union, 146
Ames, Oakes, 25
Anthony, Susan B., 26–27, 57–58
Apaches, 65–66, 70, 73, 114
Arizona Territory, 62–63, 65
Army of Northern Virginia, 16
Arthur, Chester Alan II, 57
Arthur, Malvina, 5
Arthur, William, 5
Astor, John Jacob, 45, 169

B

Baltimore, 1, 13, 26, 33, 136–37, 152
Barnum, Phineas Taylor, 155

Bayard, Thomas, 41, 118, 164–65
Beecher, Henry Ward, 45, 140, 164
Bell, Alexander Graham, 3, 150
Bell, John, 13–14
Benjamin, Samuel Green Wheeler, 132
Berlin Conference, 124–25
black civil rights, 27, 31, 72, 74
Blaine, James G., 1–2, 26, 28–29, 37–38, 44–46, 52, 107, 117–18, 121–22, 125, 127, 129, 131, 134, 144, 159–64, 166, 168–71, 174, 177
Bland-Allison Act, 93
Blatchford, Samuel, 56, 177
Bly, Nellie, 60–61
Booth, John Wilkes, 103
Booth, William, 135
Brady, John, 4, 48
Breckinridge, John, 13–14
Brewster, Benjamin, 53, 95, 177
British Columbia, 147
Brooklyn Bridge, 84–86

Brooks, James, 26

Brown, Benjamin Gratz, 25–26

Brownson, Orestes, 171, 181

Buchanan, James, ix, 13–14, 28, 97

Bullard, Robert Lee, 70

Bush, George H. W., 6

Bushnell, David, 108

Bushnell, Horace, 140

Butler, Benjamin, 166, 170

C

Carlisle Indian Industrial School, 66

Carnegie, Andrew, 98, 151, 169

Carroll, John, 136

Catholic Church, 136–38

Central America, 10, 115–16, 173

Chambers, Benjamin, 43

Chandler, William E., 53, 103–4, 106–7, 109–10, 113, 177

Chicago, 12–13, 37, 87, 107, 145, 152, 154, 161, 164

Chinese Exclusion Act, 89

Chinese immigration, 88–90

Christianity, 127, 130, 133, 140–43

Civil Service Commission, 82

Civil War, ix, 10, 19–20, 24–25, 28, 30, 40, 45, 64, 70–71, 74–75, 79, 81, 84, 88, 92, 97, 101–2, 104, 108, 110–11, 113, 122, 134, 136–37, 144, 150–51, 153, 157, 160–61, 163, 166–69, 183

Claflin, Tennessee C., 26, 60

Clayton-Bulwer Treaty, 116

Cleveland, Grover, x, 77, 81–82, 86–87, 91, 94, 97, 107–9, 117–19, 125, 159, 164–70, 173–75, 177, 181–82, 186

Codman, John, 101

Cody, William "Buffalo Bill", 62, 151

Colfax, Schuyler, 25–26

Comanche, 67–69

Communist Party, 76

Conger, Frank B., 164

Congo, the, 123–25

Congress, 23, 48, 52, 61, 64, 80, 82, 88–91, 93–95, 97–99, 101–6, 116, 121, 124, 126, 146–47, 151, 161, 174, 177, 182–83, 185

Conkling machine, 23–24, 28, 47, 80, 157

Conkling, Roscoe, x, 12, 16, 20, 23, 26, 28–29, 33–35, 37–39, 41, 43–48, 54–56, 62, 81, 159, 170, 177

Constitution, 13, 31, 51, 58–59, 69, 86, 93, 124, 147, 182–83

Constitutional Union Party, 13–14

Conwell, Russell, 134–35

Cook, James, 126

Cornell, Alonzo, 34–35, 80

Crédit Mobilier scandal, 25

Croker, Richards, 21

Crook, George, 70
Crosby, Fanny, 135
Crowley, Richard, 44–45
Cuba, 70, 105, 185
Culver, E. D., 6

D
Danish West Indies, 184,
Darwin, Charles, 141–42
Davis, David, 25, 30
Davis, Jefferson, 14, 71
Davis, Richard Harding, 114
de Lesseps, Ferdinand, 117
Democratic Party, 7, 26, 28, 71, 76, 98
Depew, Chauncey, 44
Dewey, George, 102, 111–12
Diuturnum illud, 138
Douglas, Stephen, 7, 12–14
Douglass, Frederick, 27, 74–75, 77
Du Bois, W. E. B., 75–76
Dunbar High School, 72

E
Earp, Wyatt, 62–63
Eastern Europe, 136, 140–41
Eaton, Dorman B., 82, 157
Edmunds, George, 38, 160–63
Eighteenth Amendment, 147
Electoral College, 28
Emancipation Proclamation, 17, 75
English, William H., 40, 41
Equal Rights Party, 26–27

Europe, 70, 105, 110, 114, 125–26, 136, 139–41, 143–44, 149
Everett, Edward, 13

F
Fenton, Robert, 19–20
Fifth Avenue Hotel, 86, 168
Fiske, John, 142
Flipper, Henry Ossian, 73–74
Folsom, Oscar, 167
Fort Donelson, 136
Fort Sumter, 15
Franklyn, Charles G., 3
Frelinghuysen, Frederick T., 52, 117, 121, 176

G
Gardiner, Henry G., 8
Garfield, James, ix–x, 1–4, 24, 37–39, 41, 43–44, 46–48, 52–53, 56, 71, 74, 77, 79, 94–95, 98, 102–3, 112–13, 131, 134, 136, 160–61, 175, 182, 186
George, Henry, 147–48
Georgetown College, 137
Geronimo (Goyahkla), 65–66, 70
Gibbons, James Cardinal, 137–38
Gladden, Washington, 140
Godkin, E. L., 45
Gold Standard Act, 92
Goldwater, Barry, 143
Gompers, Samuel, 88–89, 145, 174
Gordon, Charles, 174
Gould, Jay, 87, 169

Grant, Ulysses S., x, 23–29, 37–40, 43, 45, 48, 56, 81–82, 97, 102, 106, 113, 116, 129, 131, 134, 136, 159, 174–75, 182
Gray, Horace, 56
Greeley, Horace, 25–28
Greely, Adolphus, 109
Greenback Labor Party, 43, 166, 169
Greenland, 109
Gregory, John M., 82
Guano Islands Act, 126
Guiteau, Charles Julius, 2

H
Hale, Lucy, 103
Half-Breed faction, 44, 62
Halpin, Maria, 167
Hamlin, Hannibal, 13
Harvard Law School, 53, 103, 113
Harvard University, 60, 76, 113, 152–53
Hawaii, 126–28, 130
Hayes, Rutherford B., x, 28–31, 33–35, 37–38, 41, 48, 56–57, 66, 69, 74, 77, 93, 102, 116, 130, 134, 157, 176–77, 182
Hepburn v. Griswold, 93
Herndon, Ellen Lewis (Nell), 8–10, 15, 18, 35–36, 41, 52
Herndon, William, 8, 10
Holliday, John "Doc", 62

Homer, Winslow, 154
Hudson River, 1, 154
Hunt, William H., 47, 53, 103, 106, 113
Huxley, Thomas, 141

I
Illinois, 7, 12, 25, 81–82, 98, 144–45, 163
Indochina, 130
Industrial Revolution, 69
International Workingmen's Association, 26
Interstate Commerce Act, 146
Interstate Commerce Commission, 146
Ireland, 5, 86, 88, 108, 122, 136, 138

J
Jackson, Andrew, ix, 11, 31, 182
Jackson, Helen Hunt, 69
James, Thomas L., 53
Jarrett, Henry C., 150
Jennings, Lizzie, 7
Johnson, Andrew, x, 19, 28, 102–3, 182
Jones, John P., 54
Judaism, 140

K
Kalakaua, David, 127–28
Kansas-Nebraska Act, 7

Kasson, John A., 124–25, 184
Kelly, John, 21
Kernan, Francis, 44
Key, David M., 31
Kirk, Russell, 171
Knights of Columbus, the, 137
Knights of Labor, the, 87
Korea, 130–31
Krakatoa, 96

L

La Guardia, Fiorello, 21
La Flesche, Susette (Bright Eyes), 69
Lane, Joseph, 13
Latter-day Saints, 61
Lee, Robert E., 16, 19, 83
Leo XIII, Pope, 138
Leopold II, 124–25
Liggett, Hunter, 70
Lincoln Center, 154
Lincoln, Robert Todd, 45–46, 52,
    73, 112–14, 160, 162, 177–78
Lodge, Henry Cabot, 160–61,
    164
Lowell, James Russell, 25
Luce, Stephen B., 110

M

MacDowell, Edward, 154
MacVeagh, Wayne, 46, 53
Mahan, Alfred Thayer, 110–11
Maine, 1, 13, 28, 37, 146, 154
major league baseball, 72–73
Manhattan College, 152

Marine Corps, 57
Marx, Karl, 143–44
Massachusetts, 1, 13, 25–26, 74,
    80, 135, 140, 152–53, 160,
    163, 166
McClellan, George, 16, 83–84
McElroy, John, 57
McGivney, Michael J., 137
McKinley, William, 82, 94, 125,
    168, 176, 178, 182–83
Merritt, Edwin A., 35
Metropolitan Opera House, 154
Mexico, 64–65, 99, 123, 136,
    149, 174
Middle East, the, 105, 131
Miles, Nelson A., 70, 112
Missouri Compromise, 7
Monroe Doctrine, 125, 184
Moody, Dwight Lyman, 133–34
Moore, Clement Clarke, 139
Morgan, Edwin D., 12, 15–17,
    19–20, 52
Morgan, H. Wayne, 91
Morgan, J. P., 45, 98
Morgan, John T., 118, 124
Morse, Samuel, 150
Morton, Levi, 39, 44, 46
Morton, Oliver, 28–29

N

Nation, the, 45, 164
National Association of Profes-
    sional Base Ball Players, 152

National Association of Wool
    Manufacturers, 98, 174
National Football League, 153
National Guard Association, 64
National Liberal Party, 144
National Woman Suffrage, 57
Naval Academy, 106, 110–11,
    175
New Granada, 115
New Hampshire, 26, 53, 103–4
New York City, 1, 4, 6–7, 16, 18,
    20–21, 27–28, 35, 47, 56, 60,
    81, 84, 148, 153, 157, 168,
    176, 178
New York City Tax Commission,
    21
New York Herald, the, 25, 73,
    86, 150, 166, 184
New York Times, the, 48, 79, 95,
    127, 162, 164
New York Tribune, the, 86, 176
Nicaragua, 117–18, 173
North Star, the, 74
Northern Whigs, 7–8

O
O'Connor, Charles, 26
Oberlin College, 60, 73
Office of Naval Intelligence, 103
Oklahoma, 68, 74
Ottoman Empire, 136

P
Panama Canal, 115–19, 173

Panama Railroad Company, 116
Panic of 1873, 159
Panic of 1893, 94, 145, 159
Parker, Quanah, 67–69
Patterson, James, 26
Pendleton Civil Service Reform
    Act, 81–82, 185
Pendleton, George H., 82, 118
Peninsula Campaign, 16
Pershing, John J., 70, 109
Philadelphia, 25, 33, 135, 147,
    152, 154
Pierce, Franklin, ix, 7, 14
Platt, Thomas, 44–45, 47
polygamy, 61
Ponca tribe, 69
Pope, John, 16, 83
pork-barrel legislation, 88, 90–91
Porter, Fitz John, 83–84
Post Office Department, 94
Princeton, 18, 53, 142, 153, 176
Prohibition Party, 147, 166–67
Proteus, 109
Puerto Rico, 70, 105, 185
Pullman Car Company, 53, 145
Pullman, George, 145–46

R
Reconstruction, 29–30, 71–72,
    188
Reid, Whitelaw, 25
Republican National Convention,
    122, 161

Republican Party, 7–8, 12, 19–20, 24–25, 30, 33–34, 43, 48, 52, 75, 81, 178

Revolutionary War, 92

Richmond, the, 106

Rivers and Harbors Act, 88–90

Robertson, William H., 44, 47

Robinson, Jackie, 73

Rockefeller, John D., 134

Rogers, John, 103

Roosevelt, Franklin Delano, 94, 183

Roosevelt, Theodore, ix–x, 1, 6, 34, 57, 80, 82, 109–10, 119, 125, 148, 151, 160, 173, 182

Root, Elihu, 178–79

Royal Navy, 101, 108, 111–12

Russia, 2, 53, 102, 105, 125–26, 130–32, 141

S

Salvation Army, the, 135

Samoa, 126, 128–30

Sampson, William, 111–12

Schurz, Carl, 25, 66, 157, 160, 164

Scofield, Cyrus, 134

Second Battle of Bull Run, 16, 83

Selden, George, 149

Seward, William, 12–13

Seymour, Horatio, 17

Sherman Silver Purchase Act, 93–94

Sherman, John, 33, 35, 37–38, 44, 93–94, 118, 162–63

Sherman, William Tecumseh, 19, 29, 73, 81, 113, 160

Shufeldt, Robert W., 107, 130–31

slavery, 7, 10, 12–14, 17, 19, 24, 76, 83, 124

Society of Tammany, 20

South Carolina, 12, 14–15, 30–31, 71, 74

Southern Whigs, 7

Southwest Railway, 87

Spanish-American War, 64, 70, 103, 112, 161

Spencer, Herbert, 141–42

Stalwarts, the, 37, 43–45, 47, 52, 62, 157, 170

Stanton, Elizabeth Cady, 60

Stephens, Alexander, 14, 27

Sullivan, John L., 153–54

Sumner, Charles, 25, 129

Sumner, William Graham, 98, 143, 152

Sunda Strait, 96

Syphax, William, 72

T

Tammany Hall, 20–21, 165, 168

tariffs, 11, 23, 41, 97–99, 143, 166, 174, 185

Taylor, Zachary, ix, 116

Temple College (Temple University), 135

Thoman, Leroy D., 82

Thompson, Michael W., 110
Thurman, Allen G., 41, 164
Tilden, Samuel, 28, 81, 164
Tritle, Frederick A., 63
Trumbull, Lyman, 25
Turner, Frederick Jackson, 150
Tuskegee Normal and Industrial
    Institution, 72, 75
Tweed, William Meager "Boss,"
    20, 21, 28
Twenty-fifth Amendment, 86,
    183
Twenty-first Amendment, 147
Tyler, John, 14

U
U.S. House of Representatives,
    13–14, 20, 30–31, 34, 37, 43,
    80, 94, 159, 166
U.S. Navy, 53, 102–3, 107–8,
    112, 125
U.S. Supreme Court, 4, 23, 25,
    27, 30, 54, 56, 61, 93
Union Pacific, 25
Union, the, 11, 13–14, 17, 19, 24,
    61, 71, 80
United Kingdom, 2, 25, 53, 105,
    122, 129
USS *Ticonderoga*, 130–31
Utah, 27, 61, 149

V
von Bismarck, Otto, 124–25

W
Waite, Morrison, 2, 48, 175
Walker, Moses Fleetwood, 72–73
Wallace, Lew, 136
War of 1812, 97
Warfield, Benjamin B., 142
Washburne, Elihu, 38–39
Washington Post, the, 170
Washington, Booker T., 75,
Washington, George, 37
Weaver, James, 43
Weed, Thurlow, 12, 16, 20, 45
Wells, David A., 97–98
West Point, 40, 64, 70, 73–74,
    83, 111, 114
White House, 1–3, 35, 54, 56–57,
    65, 94, 134, 138, 163–64, 167,
    175, 182
Whittaker, Johnson Chesnut, 74
Willard, Frances, 147–48
Wilson, Henry, 26
Windom, William, 38, 46, 52, 98
Women's Christian Temperance
    Union, 146–47
Woodhull, Victoria, 26, 60
Woodruff, Wilford, 61
World War I, 70, 111–12, 114, 129
World War II, 112, 114, 126

Y
Yale, 6, 98, 134, 140, 143,
    152–53
Yellowstone National Park, 151
Young Men's Christian Associa-
    tion, 134